Learning

Contracts

Geoff Anderson, David Boud
Jane Sampson

**KOGAN
PAGE**

<u>YOURS TO HAVE AND TO HOLD</u>
<u>BUT NOT TO COPY</u>

The publication you are reading is protected by copyright law. This means that the publisher could take you and your employer to court and claim heavy legal damages if you make unauthorized photocopies from these pages.

Photocopying copyright material without permission is no different from stealing a magazine from a newsagent, only it doesn't seem like theft.

The Copyright Licensing Agency (CLA) is an organization which issues licenses to bring photocopying within the law. It has designed licensing services to cover all kinds of special needs in business, education and government.

If you take photocopies from books, magazines and periodicals at work your employer should be licensed with CLA. Make sure you are protected by a photocopying licence.

The Copyright Licensing Agency Limited, 90 Tottenham Court Road, London, W1P 0LP. Tel: 0171 436 5931. Fax: 0171 436 3986.

First published in 1996

Apart from any fair dealing for the purposes of research or private study, or criticism or review, as permitted under the Copyright, Designs and Patents Act, 1988, this publication may only be reproduced, stored or transmitted, in any form or by any means, with the prior permission in writing of the publishers, or in the case of reprographic reproduction in accordance with the terms and licenses issued by the CLA. Enquiries concerning reproduction outside those terms should be sent to the publishers at the undermentioned address.

Kogan Page Limited
120 Pentonville Road
London N1 9JN

© Geoff Anderson, David Boud and Jane Sampson, 1996

British Library Cataloguing in Publication Data

A CIP record for this book is available from the British Library.

ISBN 0 7494 1847 8

Typeset by Northern Phototypesetting Co Ltd, Bolton
Printed and bound in Great Britain by Clays Ltd, St Ives plc

Contents

Preface

This book is designed to introduce learning contracts to those who are considering adopting the method in their own courses. It aims to help teaching staff make decisions about how contracts may best be used and how they might relate to existing learning and assessment practices. At the same time those familiar with contracts should find the models provided and the issues discussed helpful in furthering their understanding of the method and in suggesting additional ways in which this versatile approach to organizing learning can be employed.

The book arose from our experience of using learning contracts and other forms of negotiated learning within our own courses. The school in which we teach has a major commitment to taking account of students' experience, responding to their learning needs and linking with their work or employment aspirations while they pursue their formal study. Our undergraduate students will have typically negotiated over 50 learning contracts by the time they graduate. Learning contracts have been used in the school for 17 years. This means that there is a considerable body of expertise on which to draw.

Our interest in negotiated learning led us to undertake a programme of research and teaching development to tap into this experience. We aimed to ascertain what teachers and students regarded as good practice in the use of learning contracts, identify what was required to introduce learning contracts effectively, and develop materials and conduct training activities to improve practice.

The materials we produced to support workshops were well regarded by participants and we responded to a large number of requests for copies from other institutions. This led us to consider extending the local guides into a book which would address wider concerns. Hence the present volume.

Part I of the book is introductory. It outlines the basic concepts needed to understand the method and describes the process involved in developing a fully negotiated learning contract. Part II discusses the various components of a typical learning contract in more detail and is intended to serve as a reference during the contracting process. Part III addresses the question of how to introduce learning contracts into a course for the first time and considers the needs of teachers, students and those managing departments.

Part IV suggests how the basic model can be adapted to suit different purposes, different courses and different situations. Although learning contracts are usually negotiated between an individual learner and an adviser, in many courses contracts are developed with groups of students, or with pairs of students, or with a third party, such as a workplace supervisor.

The book concludes by taking a more critical perspective emphasizing that while the use of learning contracts can be a useful teaching and learning strategy, it is not an educational panacea. For those who wish to read further, the bibliography lists a number of publications dealing with learning contracts in general, how they are used in particular courses and other issues relating to this type of learning and assessment.

Throughout this book we have used the term 'learning contract', but it is important to note that it does not imply a legal document but rather a negotiated plan or agreement that certain activities will occur and that certain results will be produced in exchange for assessment credit. The terms 'learning agreement' or 'learning plan' are sometimes preferred. Unlike some forms of individualized learning, a learning contract puts responsibility on the learner, often with few prepared activities, resources or programmes being directly provided. Apart from making the learning personally meaningful to each student, the process also aims to develop the skills and initiative students need to meet their learning needs long after the course has finished.

There has been particular interest in negotiated learning in recent years. There are many reasons for this, such as an increase in the number of mature age and part-time students undertaking further study, the demand for greater student input into what is to be studied and the fact that many professional courses now include a significant work experience component. Teachers can see advantages in the method's flexibility. Learning contracts can respond to the diverse needs of learners from different backgrounds while still maintaining standards expected in an accredited course. When implemented well, they are popular with both students and teachers.

Contract learning has been successfully implemented in courses as diverse as education, business management, computer science, electrical engineering, history, medicine, mechanical engineering, nursing, physiotherapy and social work. It has been used at all post-secondary levels in small colleges as well as major universities.

It would be wrong to claim learning contracts are suitable for all courses or can be used with all types of learners. The method can be adapted to a wide range of subject areas but like any other learning strategy it needs to be used appropriately and with awareness of its limitations. The discussion in this book should help readers make an informed decision about the adoption and use of learning contracts in their particular context.

Acknowledgments

The original version of this guide was produced with the support of the Australian Committee for the Advancement of University Teaching through a National Teaching Development Grant. We would like to thank staff and students from the University of Technology, Sydney who have contributed ideas and information for the guide. In particular we acknowledge the contributions of academic staff from the Faculty of Education who responded to our survey regarding the qualities staff look for in both the contract proposals and the completed work and all those students who completed our questionnaire regarding student experiences with contracts.

Thanks also to our students Liane Beattie, Jenny Dixon-Elliott, David Gray, Judy McCormick, Clive McPartland, Barbie Pemberton and Ian Webb for their investigations and reflections about how students use contracts and to Cynthia Borthwick, Ruth Cohen, Patricia Farrer, Trevor Habeshaw, Joy Higgs, Susan Knights, Jo McKenzie, Jeff Rolls, Susan Shannon, Keith Trigwell, Mark Tennant and Peter Younger who provided valuable comments on the original draft of the guide. Some material in Chapter 3 draws on ideas contained in a handbook for students prepared originally by Geoff Scott and material in Chapter 11 draws on ideas introduced to students by Susan Knights and Griff Foley.

We would like to thank all those from other faculties and universities who have shared their ideas and experiences with us at workshops, conferences and in conversation. In particular we acknowledge the examples of learning contracts provided by Vinette Cross, Queen Elizabeth School of Physiotherapy, Birmingham; Bob Gowing, School of Adult Education, University of Technology, Sydney; Clive Mathews and Helen McGregor, School of Mechanical Engineering, University of Technology, Sydney; Susan Neville, Faculty of Science and Health, University of East London; Marilyn Place, Department of Physiotherapy Studies, University of Keele; Cedric Richardson, School of Computing Sciences, University of Technology, Sydney; and Elizabeth Taylor, School of Electrical Engineering, University of Technology, Sydney.

We particularly appreciate the encouragement given to us to turn our ideas into a book by John Stephenson of Higher Education for Capability and the very helpful comments of our colleague Mike Newman on an earlier draft of the book.

Finally, no book on learning contracts could be complete without reference to the enormous influence of Malcolm Knowles in shaping thinking in this area. Through his writing, his workshops and his personal influence he has perhaps done more to move practice in higher education towards a learner-centred view than any other person. Even in the UK where his work is surprisingly little cited, his influence is apparent through the adoption of forms of negotiated learning for which he has been the original major advocate. It has now become popular in some quarters to be dismissive of approaches to learning which focus on the individual rather than on a broader conception of the learning context, but without the awareness that Knowles and others have brought to teaching, we might still be tempted to underemphasize the importance of the key person in the learning process – the learner.

Geoff Anderson, David Boud
and Jane Sampson
School of Adult Education,
University of Technology, Sydney
November 1995

PART I

INTRODUCTION

Chapter 1

What is a learning contract?

A learning contract is a document used to assist in the planning of a learning project. It is a written agreement negotiated between a learner and a teacher, lecturer or staff adviser that a particular activity will be undertaken in order to achieve a specific learning goal or goals.

The use of learning contracts is based upon a number of assumptions about the nature of learning and learners. It derives largely from the ideas of educators such as Malcolm Knowles who believe that as autonomous human beings, adult learners should be encouraged to take more responsibility for their own learning and to use their existing skills and experiences as the basis for new learning, and that they should also be allowed in formal educational settings to learn things which are of importance to them. While Knowles originally focused on adult learners studying in tertiary education institutions, the use of learning contracts has now spread to primary and secondary schools, to vocational training and to staff development in many organizations.

A flexible method

This approach may at first seem at odds with the conventional view that students attend a course to receive knowledge and that the lecturer or teacher is the subject expert who determines what and how they will learn. But even in these traditional courses, based around lectures, classroom presentations, set assignments and formal examinations, a learning contract can be a useful adjunct to other methods of teaching and assessing students. It offers many benefits, not least student commitment, which can more than compensate for any perceived drawbacks. Even in highly technical subjects the method can be an interesting way to cover selected topics or to encourage students to engage in more in-depth learning. A great advantage of the method is its flexibility. It is a mistake to think of learning contracts as applicable only to certain disciplines or for use only with certain types of learners. As the following chapters will show, the basic method can be adapted into virtually any teaching or training area and into at least part of any course. It is a useful means of extending and enhancing existing teaching practices in any setting.

Knowles *et al.* (1986) emphasizes the fact that a learning contract is essentially a 'process plan'. It is a means of designing a learning activity with the focus on the learner rather than the subject or the teacher. For this reason learning contracts are particularly suitable for structuring assignments and projects which are largely self-directed, for use in courses in which participants come from a diversity of backgrounds and in tailoring learning to individual needs and interests. They can also be used where assignments might traditionally be used, or they can form the structure for whole courses of study.

The role of the adviser

A learning contract, or negotiated learning agreement as it is sometimes called, implies a degree of negotiation and commitment by at least two parties – the learner and the staff member representing an educational institution. This staff member could be a course coordinator, a subject lecturer, a tutor, teacher, instructor, or a postgraduate supervisor. Since job titles such as 'lecturer' and 'supervisor' have existing meanings and imply a particular view of learning, the term 'adviser' is used here to describe the role this person performs, regardless of their position title.

Negotiated learning normally begins with some discussion as to the roles, responsibilities and expectations of the parties concerned. These will vary according to such factors as the background and experience of the learner and the level of the course, but essentially the learner is responsible for completing the agreed activities and the adviser for offering the necessary support and ensuring the course requirements are being met. The process is very much one of negotiation and consensus-seeking.

To agree upon the nature of the learning project requires a collaborative relationship based upon open communications and a degree of mutual respect. It is here that the first difficulty may arise, especially if either the learner or the adviser come from a strongly instrumental background (this would include students who have been trained to pass traditional examinations based on a prescribed curriculum). The first task may well be to address the frame of reference that the learner brings to the course and to change the emphasis from completing a course requirement to meeting a learning need. While the responsibility for the project ultimately rests with the learner, ongoing consultations may occur throughout the project and the adviser will at times have to balance support and assistance with the need to maintain direction, relevance and educational standards. The exact level of ongoing support and advice is governed as much by overall resource constraints as by educational considerations.

Successful learning contracts often involve a return to dialogue to enable the learner to reflect upon learning to date and to discuss future directions. Ongoing monitoring and support are a normal part of the adviser's role. Still, it is important that the learner feels ownership of the contract and any suggestion that he or she is merely agreeing to do things suggested or imposed by the adviser should, of course, be avoided. Some careful balancing is needed here because at the same time the adviser should be aiming to challenge and extend the learner and be satisfied that new learning is occurring or new skills being developed. These will usually extend beyond the specific content area of the topic to encompass communication, organization, time management, and product presentation skills. In contract learning, the process is as much a part of the learning experience as the content.

Since learners seldom have identical goals or objectives, the role of the staff adviser becomes more critical than in other modes of teaching. The adviser will be attempting to balance the needs and preferences of the student with the requirements of the course. The adviser's role is therefore both supportive and evaluative.

In summary, a learning contract is a negotiated agreement based upon both the learning needs of the individual undertaking the contract as well as the formal requirements of the course or institution involved. It is a plan of action as much as a statement of expected outcomes. Its value lies in its relevance and application to the needs of each learner.

Elements of a learning contract

The exact format of a learning contract may vary slightly from one course to another and various models are available to suit different purposes. However a typical contract is divided into four separate sections. These sections detail:

- the learning objectives or goals of the project
- the strategies and resources available to achieve these objectives
- the evidence which will be produced to indicate the objectives have been achieved
- the criteria which will be used to assess this evidence.

In addition, the contract will usually specify a commencement and completion date for the project and may also indicate which particular competences or areas of knowledge the contract is addressing. Once the details have been agreed to by both the learner and the adviser each party signs the document and retains a copy. Figure 1.1 provides an example of a typical learning contract form.

Often the adviser will write comments or suggestions on the contract (some contracts have a separate section for this purpose) or the learner may record points arising from discussions.

If the original contract needs to be renegotiated, amendments or revisions can be made and initialled during subsequent discussions. It is important that, in keeping with the spirit of the learning contract method, any changes are mutually agreed. The success of the completed work is usually judged in terms of how well it meets the agreed objectives, hence discussion needs to occur if the objectives are to be changed or varied in any way, regardless of whether it is the adviser or someone else who actually assesses the completed work.

Academic rigour versus learner support

The negotiated learning contract lies somewhere along a continuum which has a totally prescribed task at one end and a fully independent, self-directed learning activity at the other. While it is convenient to think of the learning contract as a type of project management plan for the self-directed learner, in reality it is developed within parameters, sometimes quite rigid, imposed by the staff adviser as a representative of the accrediting body. Within an educational setting, the learning contract is used as much as a formal assessment activity as a learning plan. Indeed, a learning contract can never be fully self-directed since the very act of negotiating the learning naturally involves another person.

The act of negotiation implies a process of give and take in which each party is prepared to concede some points in return for others. While the learner has more control than is usual, there still remain areas not open to negotiation. Experts on negotiation stress that while a willingness to compromise is essential to a successful agreement being reached, there will also be points which are non-negotiable and which the individual will not be prepared to concede. Knowing what is and what is not negotiable and clarifying this during the initial discussion is an important stage in designing a suitable learning contract. This area of non-negotiation normally centres on assessment criteria and features of the curriculum which may be standard for all learners undertaking a particular course (see Chapter 7).

A major role for the adviser is ensuring the contract meets the academic requirements of the institution concerned and is appropriately rigorous. Hence the advice, guidance and amount of personal support offered will

LEARNING CONTRACT PROPOSAL FORM

Student/s: **Subject:**

Adviser: **Competency area or topic:**

Date agreed: **Date due:**

Learning Objectives	Strategies and Resources	What is to be Assessed	Criteria for Assessment

Signature of student:

Contact (student) phone: Fax:

Signature of adviser:

Contact (adviser) phone: Fax:

Figure 1.1 Example of a typical learning contract form

sometimes need to be tempered by these considerations. The limits of support and the bounds of freedom need to be discussed at an early stage.

How do contracts and set assignments differ?

There is an important difference between negotiating a learning contract and undertaking a set assignment. Unlike an assignment, a learning contract is a document based upon discussion and shared decision making. The contract is open to renegotiation if circumstances change. This needs to be recognized from the outset. Learners drafting a learning contract for the first time usually spend a lot of time worrying about 'getting it right' yet if the contract is viewed as a working document rather than a binding commitment much of this early anxiety can be avoided.

When students and staff are being introduced to learning contracts, especially if they are being used within an existing course or programme, it can be helpful to situate them within a more familiar framework. For example, defining the differences between a learning contract and a set assignment, and explaining the rationale for its use in terms of its contribution to student learning.

It is also important to note that learning contracts are seldom the only method of learning and assessment used throughout a course, although they may be exclusively used in a particular subject or module. More commonly, other tasks, activities and assignments are given to complement contracts and to ensure all important areas of the curriculum are covered and essential skills and knowledge acquired.

Since it is used for both learning and assessment purposes there may also be some confusion about where a learning contract should be placed within a course. Is the contract being used mainly as an alternative learning methodology or as an assessment activity? Staff and students need to be clear about the purpose of the contract and just how far it can go in meeting the range of learning which the course covers. For example, a single contract may not always be sufficient to adequately assess a learner's mastery of a particular subject. Decisions about whether or not to use learning contracts will need to be made with an understanding of how best to use them and whether to base final assessment solely on the completed contract or on other evidence as well.

A learning contract is like a project plan in so far as it identifies an objective and the means to achieve it. In this case the objective is a new area of skill or knowledge which the learner wishes to develop. The contract is like a traditional assignment in that it will be assessed and evaluated in terms of how well it has met specified criteria. In a fully self-directed learning activity this assessment component is normally either not present or not so important,

7

since learner satisfaction becomes the major criterion of success (Caffarella and O'Donnell, 1991).

However a contract is more than simply a 'free choice of topic' assignment. While it may be used within a particular subject or course and neither the process nor the product is prescribed in advance, the contract takes shape following an analysis of individual learning needs and a consideration of the most useful ways of meeting those needs. If writing an essay or report is not considered particularly useful, other options can be explored. The method allows for considerable freedom and flexibility in determining both what is to be submitted for assessment and how it will be produced.

The completed contract

It is difficult to talk in general terms about the outcomes of learning contracts since their form can vary considerably from one context to another. One learner in one course may contract to write a book review while another in a different course writes a book. One produces a video, another writes a critique of a television programme. The length may range from a 500-word essay to a 5,000-word report or there may be no length restrictions at all. The contract may be limited to topics relevant to a particular subject within a course or it may form the basis for a course in its own right.

Some courses provide learners with the opportunity to explore areas outside the set subjects by means of an independent learning contract or an individualized project for which credit is granted. In this case learners have considerable freedom to select topics based on their own interests at the time. It would be expected, of course, that the contract would relate to the main theme of the formal course.

However it is used, the 'average' learning contract, once submitted for assessment, may look a lot like a set assignment. Learners base their contracts on topics relevant to the subject being studied, usually following the suggestions and advice of the subject lecturer or other staff adviser. They will most typically choose to write an essay or a report. All very familiar. But while set assignments can vary, contracts can sometimes be even more varied, especially in terms of their aims and objectives. The whole idea of using a negotiated learning contract is to allow each learner the opportunity to work in an area relevant to his or her own personal needs and interests.

Further learning

A significant feature of contract learning is its potential to promote deep approaches to learning (Marton *et al.*, 1984). When well prepared, learners are encouraged to go beyond assembling subject knowledge to consider how this knowledge may actually be acquired, what it may mean to them, how successful their learning has been and what further implications it may hold. The contract method can stimulate learners to examine their own assumptions, beliefs and learning preferences, to be more reflective about their work, and to work collaboratively. Collaboration in the learning process may involve just one other person (the adviser) or it may involve working as a member of a small group of learners on a project of mutual interest. So while the contract will be explicit about the content of the topics to be studied it also implies 'subtler agreement about values, assumptions and ideals' (Hansen, 1991: 123).

The contract objectives may choose to emphasize product, process or reflective evaluation (Russell *et al.*, 1994). Typically all three components will be present, each being emphasized at different stages during the life of the contract. It is here that both the learner and the adviser are engaged in mutually constructing the educational experience. Rather than being a passive recipient of knowledge the learner is forced to take a more active and subjective role. By taking the initiative for the learning project, the learner is more likely to engage in deeper and more lasting learning.

While they can be used in most subjects, learning contracts are particularly suited to courses which include some practical component, such as work experience programmes, or which make use of problem-based learning or other learner-centred strategies. This is due to the freedom they offer the learner to organize resources and available learning opportunities to meet a determined learning need. The learner is actively engaged in exploring the potential for learning in situations which may otherwise be overlooked. For deep approaches to learning to occur, it is important that the contract be carefully constructed. The main stages in the actual process of developing a learning contract are described in Chapter 3.

Later, in Chapter 8, examples of learning contracts from different courses are discussed. The examples are intended to indicate the type of information which is provided in each part of the contract and provide an indication of the variety of contract styles which are possible.

Chapter 2

Why use learning contracts?

Without question the single most potent tool I have come across in my more than half-century of experience with adult education is contract learning.

Malcolm Knowles (1990: 127)

Even today, learning contracts are regarded as a fairly innovative way of undertaking a learning project or supplementing formal course work, particularly when they are used for assessment within an award programme. When first introduced to the idea learners are naturally curious about the reasons for using learning contracts. While the benefits may differ from one individual to another, experience over many years in a variety of different courses suggests certain basic advantages.

Reasons for using learning contracts

Relevance

Learning contracts acknowledge individual differences and enable learning activities to be tailored to the specific needs and interests of each learner. They provide a means of reconciling a learner's personal needs with the formal assessment requirements of an educational institution or other accrediting body. Since students have identified their own learning needs the activities are likely to be more meaningful, relevant and interesting for them. Hence motivation and commitment are likely to be higher than with traditional learning and assessment methods (Smith, 1983).

In professional and continuing education contexts, learning contracts can be used to develop specific skills and competences relevant to each learner's own work or field of practice. Contracts build on and develop the existing skills and experience of the learner, recognizing connections and sequences.

Thus learning is made more immediate and applicable than may otherwise be the case. This in turn has a considerable motivating effect on the learner.

Autonomy

Learning how to learn is a major part of any educational process. Learning contracts encourage learners to take responsibility for their own learning and become less dependent upon direction from others. They allow considerable freedom of choice in terms of what to learn and how to learn it. The learning contract allows them to take an active role in the total learning process, from setting objectives to designing learning strategies and finally to evaluating outcomes.

In addition to content knowledge, learners can develop many generic skills in areas such as objective setting, communication and negotiation, project planning and project evaluation. These are vocational competences important in all fields of professional practice. Learners are also more likely to consider or be introduced to a wider range of resources, activities and alternative approaches than is usually the case with traditional assignments or with assessments based mainly on examinations.

Students using learning contracts progressively become less dependent upon teachers and better able to continue to address their learning needs after the course has finished. By considering their own learning strategies and processes students develop a better understanding of the nature of learning and their own preferred learning approaches. The process of negotiating and completing a learning contract encourages students to reflect upon their learning and consider its application. They are therefore more likely to use analytical and reflective approaches to learning than when an assignment is imposed .

Staff advisers may well become learning partners with students. The relationship is potentially more democratic than in traditional teacher-student modes. Both can expect to gain new knowledge and new perspectives as a result of the process.

Structure

Learning contracts provide a formal framework for structuring learning activities. The need to negotiate appropriate learning objectives and strategies serves to focus learning and provide clear goals and directions. By documenting plans, outcomes and assessment criteria in advance, all interested parties (learners, advisers, institutions, employers or field supervisors) can have similar expectations of the learning project. This helps to prevent the disagreements or misinterpretations which can sometimes occur in conventional project work. At the same time contracts provide a high degree of flexibility for both learners and advisers throughout the learning process.

Equity

Learning contracts can foster an awareness of individual and cultural differences and be tailored to suit individual needs. They enable educational institutions and training providers to respond to the diverse needs of a wide range of students and the contexts in which they operate and hence promote improved access and equity within their courses. The method is also an excellent way to cater for those who, for whatever reason, cannot attend regular classes.

The context of learning contracts

Educational approaches such as negotiated learning, learning contracts and related ideas, represent a movement away from the traditional teacher-student relationship and the classroom, towards the world in which people live and work. These non-traditional approaches have not developed of their own accord. They are responses to the broader context of education and training and the social forces which influence these. There appear to be a number of factors which have combined in recent years to lead educators to critically examine their teaching approaches and consider alternatives. These factors have made higher education institutions more receptive to learner-centred approaches than was previously the case. Factors which have created a learner and learning-centred context include:

- greater participation in education by mature age and other non-traditional students
- an increase in the number of courses which include a significant work experience component
- initiatives such as Higher Education for Capability and Enterprise in Higher Education in the UK (Stephenson and Weil, 1992) which promote active, experiential and collaborative learning
- demands by students for more participation in course design
- a move away from transmissive modes of teaching towards more experiential styles
- the competency debate in higher and further education and industry
- demands by employers for graduates with better communication, interpersonal and problem-solving skills
- expansion of student numbers in all sectors and the resultant increased demands made on resources and staff
- competition for funds and a vigorous marketing of higher education courses
- a general social expectation that there should be more consultation and participation by people in decisions which affect their lives.

The role of educational institutions is now to offer opportunities which are perceived to be relevant and responsive to the needs of both students and society as a whole. This means that in the future there should be more scope for teachers and educational institutions to incorporate learning contracts into their courses. Their use in business and industry is well established, particularly in management development and performance management schemes.

Limitations

Despite their advantages learning contracts can also present a number of problems, particularly in the early stages of their use. As Brookfield (1985) has observed, the ability to plan and write contracts is a learned skill and not some innate ability that all learners possess.

It is easy for experienced advisers to perceive the advantages of learning contracts but these are not always so obvious to new learners. In fact the freedom and flexibility contracts offer can be a source of considerable initial stress to those who may be unfamiliar with the method. In such cases it is important that the learner be guided step by step through the process. The initial orientation is therefore a vital part of the whole process since the way in which the learner is introduced to the idea of a learning contract will play a large part in the subsequent effectiveness of the method for that individual.

All advisers who have negotiated contracts with new learners can testify to the anxiety and frustration which so often accompanies the initial discussion. In fact drafting the contract proposal is seen by some learners as a major assignment in its own right!

Some general concerns

Various objections are often raised by teachers when the idea is first introduced although the basic idea is sufficiently flexible for different forms of contract learning to be used in different settings (see Chapters 14 and 15). Some of these objections are based on misconceptions of what learning contracts involve, others can be addressed through effective implementation. Some commonly expressed concerns and responses to them are discussed below:

Learners are not always in the best position to judge what they need to learn.
In which case there is a need to provide more detailed guidelines or to restrict the choice of topic area in some way. One suggestion is to specify those learning objectives which all learners must achieve, so that what remains to be negotiated in the learning contract is how these learning objectives are to be achieved and what will be assessed. When learning contracts

are not specified in this way it is the role of the adviser to help the learner decide what is likely to be a useful and relevant area in which to develop a learning contract.

Many learners simply don't know what they don't know.
If the subject is totally new to the learner, advisers will need to ensure that areas of interest and/or need are identified in accordance with the aims and objectives of the subject syllabus. Explanations and materials which provide an overview of the field may be needed. Full discussion based upon the adviser's knowledge of the subject should occur before any contract proposal is drafted. A final contract may not emerge until some weeks into the course. If the learner's previous experience does not provide sufficient background to describe a learning objective, a more prescriptive approach may be called for initially.

Some subjects do not lend themselves to the use of learning contracts.
Usually it is the teaching method, not the subject, that is the real issue here. However, in the early stages of a new course, particularly one with a high information component, the learning contracts method may not be appropriate. One option is to restrict the type of contract a learner may negotiate (this is discussed more fully in Chapter 14).

The process is very time-consuming.
Whether the learning is negotiated in a group or one-to-one, having a student engage in the additional step of planning learning can add time to the process for both adviser and learner. Howevr, the additional involvement leads to additional learning, both about the subject in questions and of academic skills. Experience suggests at least half an hour is needed for learner and adviser to negotiate a contract when doing so for the first time. Alternatives, such as the learner completing a draft proposal prior to the first meeting, using colleagues to discuss possible proposals, or the adviser dictating sections of the contract, may save time but care needs to be taken to ensure that the benefits of using negotiated contracts are not eliminated in the process.

Learners may experience problems with their advisers.
There may be little or no choice for the learner regarding which adviser is allocated. When negotiations are one-to-one and there is no cohort of peers to provide backing and support, the learner may feel vulnerable if disagreements arise. An additional problem may arise when the adviser does not have the subject expertise to offer the required level of guidance. If difficulties cannot be resolved through discussion, it may be necessary for the learner to be assigned to a new adviser (if possible) or for another staff member to be called in to offer further advice or arbitrate a dispute.

Learners and staff may resist a new method of assessment.
Any new way of doing things may produce early anxiety, especially when it is associated with assessment. Since learning contracts require teachers and learners to adopt new ways of relating, there exists the potential for discomfort. Teachers may be reluctant to relinquish power and control to the learner, while learners may expect the teacher, as the subject matter expert, to be much more directive. Learning how to work with contracts may take some time and effort for both. The support of colleagues and administrators helps, although the idea of contract learning may have to be introduced systematically into existing programmes.

Academic standards will fall if learners choose their own assessment.
There is no reason why a learning contract should be any less demanding than a set assignment or any less academically rigorous than other types of assessment. By having advisers agree to assessment criteria in advance learners are in a better position to know what is required of them in terms of acceptable work. In any case some assessment criteria, as discussed in Chapter 7, will normally be non-negotiable.

It is difficult to establish parity between learners and advisers.
Since learners are working on individually negotiated projects and since different advisers may have negotiated different outcomes, the issue of consistency and reliability of assessments naturally occurs. For this reason assessment criteria need to be established across courses and non-negotiable requirements made clear. In other words, a minimum standard in terms of quality and quantity needs to be established which will apply to all contracts submitted within a particular course. While the contract specifies what the learner will do, it does not usually indicate what role the adviser will play. Here the course coordinator or department head has a responsibility to brief advisers and monitor the process to ensure consistency.

Learning contracts are based on an outcome-oriented view of learning.
Although many contracts are written in performance or outcome terms, it is not always necessary to specify a precise end-point in order to develop a contract. A learning objective may be based upon an intended goal or activity and may even change once the learning process is underway. The main requirement is to develop a focus based upon the learner's interests and concerns at the time and the formal requirements of the course. Naturally the more specific the objective, the easier it will be to plan the learning activities and agree upon assessment criteria. This issue will be considered further in Chapter 4.

Learning contracts are too individualistic and make students self-centred.
By responding too much to their immediate needs, there is a danger that learners may ignore areas which they do not currently identify as significant for themselves. They may also tend to disregard the needs of others or avoid

collaborative learning with peers. However, a key component of the process is discussion and negotiation. While this occurs to a greater or lesser extent depending upon the learner's level of confidence and experience, the need to accommodate the views of the adviser and the requirements of the course must always be taken into account. There is also the possibility within the method for learners to work collaboratively in pairs or small groups. The contract method can make learners more critical in their approach to their other studies and more independent in thinking about what is important to them. Learning contracts are seldom intended to be the only way learners work. A trap to avoid is having a course in which all learning is undertaken in an individualistic mode. However, this danger can be found in traditional approaches just as much as those which involve learning contracts.

Problems with advisers and how contracts are used can normally be resolved as they arise, although an outside party, such as an overall coordinator will be required to provide consistency and guidance at times. Even the most enthusiastic proponent of learning contracts, Malcolm Knowles, admits that contracts are not really suitable if the subject is totally new to the learner or if the aim is simply to develop some very specific skills, such as psychomotor or interpersonal skills. However it is hard to argue that this must always be the case, given the potential of the method. An enthusiastic student and a supportive and knowledgeable adviser can often devise learning strategies to cover most situations, especially as more directed forms of skill training can be incorporated into the overall framework of a contract if required.

Chapter 3

Steps in developing a learning contract

There is no one model of a learning contract suitable for all purposes. A contract may be a simple proforma setting out the details of a short course activity or a complex project management plan for a piece of work extending over many months. Similarly, the steps involved in developing learning contracts can be modified as learners become more experienced in their use. The decision on how best to proceed ultimately rests jointly with each learner and the adviser who is supporting or assessing the project.

The following example is based upon the model originally proposed by Malcolm Knowles (1975) which seems to have broad suitability in a range of educational settings. Other options exist for other contexts (for example, work experience programmes). These are discussed in Chapters 14 and 15.

Step 1: Establish a relevant learning need

At the outset, some learning needs will be known only to the learner (eg, those related to personal goals and interests), others only to the staff adviser (eg, what all learners are expected to cover for this subject) and others will be known to both. A further category is those needs which are not apparent at the negotiation stage but which will emerge as the contract progresses (eg, the need to uncover related information or develop a skill which is needed to accomplish the desired outcome). Initial discussion should be designed to explore these various types of perceived needs before planning any specific learning objectives. In other words, the discussion will seek to identify what the learner *wants* to learn, what the learner *could* learn and what the learner *should* learn (Cross, 1992).

Establishing the learning need may be done in any number of ways but learners often benefit from some initial stimulus. Course materials, class activities and group discussions can all be used to good effect at this stage. Knowles *et al.* (1986) suggests learners draft their ideas for a contract proposal and review these in peer groups of three or four. The feedback received is likely to be more critical and confronting than that usually provided by teaching staff. This may be because staff are more prepared to accept the learner's claims as true or may be afraid of discouraging the learner if they are too critical at this stage. In any case, discussion with fellow learners, in small groups or with the whole class, is an excellent stimulus to thought about possible areas in which to develop a contract.

The learner is now in a position to discuss this need with an adviser. Establishing a genuine learning need relevant to the course requirements may take some time and advisers are cautioned against simply accepting the first idea that the learner suggests. Early ideas may be valid but they may also be just an attempt to conform to their perceptions of the adviser's expectations rather than a need of their own. Any perceived need must also be viewed in context, for example in terms of the learner's previous experience, the level and stage of the course, the nature of the contract to be developed and the overall assessment criteria.

Another useful approach is one which has been used successfully by the University of East London with new students enrolling in its Enterprise in Higher Education programme. The questions are general enough to be used by course advisers as a starting point for assessing prior learning, planning a degree programme or negotiating a specific learning contract. In fact the same questions can be asked, with increasing degrees of sophistication, at all levels of the course (Stephenson and Laycock, 1993).

Where have I been?
This invites the student to reflect upon previous education, work and life experiences. It addresses such questions as: What do I already know? What things am I good at? What has been my experience to date? What skills do I already possess which may help me in this course?

Where am I now?
Here the student is asked to honestly evaluate strengths and weaknesses in knowledge, skill and experience.

Where do I want to go?
This step requires the student to consider long-term goals and specific objectives for the programme of study. It could include such questions as: Where is my career heading? What do I really want to learn about? What skills do I wish to develop? What are my main interests? What are my goals and ambitions? How will this course help me?

Once these issues have been considered there are several sources which could be used in making a decision about specific learning needs and hence what learning contracts might be developed.

The lecture and seminar programmes.
Important sources of ideas for learning contracts are the lecture and seminar programmes in the course. During the lecture sessions on a particular topic a learner might decide to take advantage of the information and handouts provided in lectures and create a learning contract which, for example, develops the key ideas further, explores different points of view about the topic or which examines in more detail a particular theorist or school of thought.

Workshops, tutorials and readings.
During any course learners should expect to be exposed to many ideas, theories and points of view different to their own. Some of these will come from the other participants through workshops and tutorials, others from their own reading of the recommended books and journal articles. They may wish to explore some of these ideas more fully, particularly if they are likely to be useful in their own professional development. Investigating new techniques, alternative models or different ways of doing things can be valuable options for a learning contract. Alternatively, a learning contract may be based upon a theoretical issue or argue a point of view about an issue. In this case the need to develop the topic in a logical and coherent manner would become an important assessment criterion.

Research projects.
In some courses learners may become involved in a research project either by themselves or with a small group of fellow students or staff. This project could then form the basis for a learning contract provided it was relevant to the course and represented new learning for the individual involved.

Competency standards.
Many industry bodies have developed competency standards for the work performed within their industry. Various professions and occupations also have sets of competency standards and some post-secondary courses are now competency-based. These competences reflect the skills and knowledge required to perform work to an acceptable standard. By consulting an appropriate set of competences, learners may be able to identify areas in which they will need to develop their own levels of skills and knowledge.

With a staff adviser the learners relate the workplace or course competences to their own particular learning needs and together draft learning contracts to ensure these needs will be met. This usually involves a number of activities over a period of time. The course work may also need to be combined with some practical experience, for example through vacation work or field placements, to ensure a comprehensive coverage of the relevant competences.

Current work, activities and interests.
Many students work part-time (or full-time, and study part-time) or engage

in some other activities which could be used to develop learning contracts. For students who are employed, a useful source of learning needs is tasks they are required to perform in their day-to-day work, or problems which may be occurring (eg conflict within a work group). If the student is about to undertake a work experience programme, the possible learning needs can be related to the opportunities this presents or to the areas the programme is intended to cover. Alternatively, some students might identify learning needs associated with their future career paths or they may wish to acquire specific skills to assist in securing employment. Other activities, such as community or volunteer work, frequently present many learning opportunities which may be relevant to a particular course.

However, it is important to realize that a learning contract represents a new learning experience. For this reason it is normally not sufficient merely to reproduce something that has been prepared in a work context. The student must be able to demonstrate that something has actually been learnt from the experience and that this learning forms part of their course of study as well as their employment. This could be done by providing an evaluation or critical analysis of the work or by relating it to ideas or theories encountered in the course or through other readings.

Topical issues.
In all fields there are many current and emerging issues about which learners should be informed. Identifying an issue which is considered important could provide a starting point for an interesting learning contract. For example, a contract could be used to analyse the implications of a recent government decision or consider how policy changes will affect the type of functions that are performed in a field of practice. Of course, this will involve more than idle speculation. The writer would be expected to substantiate any conclusions with a reasoned argument and by references to relevant literature.

Step 2: Refine the learning need into specific objectives

Having identified a relevant learning need, the next step is to refine this need into specific and realistic objectives. It is important at this stage to realize this involves identifying a *learning intention*, not stating what will be done to achieve it or what the final product is likely to be. Thus objectives such as '*To write a report about ...*' or '*To read books about ...*' are not appropriate since they fail to identify the learning intention.

It may help at this point for the learner to think fairly broadly about what it is that he or she hopes to achieve, in other words to identify an overall purpose or rationale for the contract. Developing some general goals helps to focus the discussion and give a sense of direction to the planning which follows. The goal could be, for example, to develop more confidence in dealing with difficult clients, to learn more about the practice of a given culture or to find out more about a particular theory or concept. The goal can then be analysed further and refined into more specific learning objectives.

The objectives should reflect the learner's perceived needs but they must also be manageable and achievable given the time and resources available. There is no point in developing a learning contract that is either too ambitious to complete or is not meeting a real need on the part of the learner. The objectives should be clear and precise and represent a worthwhile learning activity, particularly if the contract will later be assessed for credit in a course.

As an example, a learner may have decided that business planning is something she would like to know more about. Rather than attempting to cover all aspects of this topic she might, in consultation with her adviser, decide to look at what some major writers in the field see as the key issues in long-term strategic planning and then prepare a hypothetical strategic plan for an actual organization. She could then focus on this particular organization as a case study when discussing the components of a strategic plan. This student is now in a good position to specify her precise learning objectives. For example:

- to identify the key components of a strategic business plan;
- to analyse the most common problems encountered when preparing a strategic plan;
- to discuss the issues involved in preparing a long-term plan for the XYZ Company;
- to prepare a strategic plan for the XYZ Company for the next five years.

Step 3: Identify useful resources and strategies for learning

The next step is to identify the best resources available to enable the learner to achieve the stated objectives. Here it is important to consider not only printed material, such as books and journals, but whatever or whoever might be able to help the learner to find out what he or she wishes to know. This could include *people* such as teachers, librarians, other students and practitioners, as well as *material* contained in sources such as books, journals, reports and the broadcast media.

There is also a need to consider the various *strategies* which may be employed to obtain the information and materials required. In other words, having identified sources of information, the learner must decide the best methods of accessing those sources. This involves working out a plan of action to determine:

- what to look for,
- who to talk to and how to approach them,
- how to locate or acquire relevant materials,
- the priorities for the project,
- a sequence in which to do things.

The adviser will be of considerable assistance at this point. Even if unable to offer specific suggestions for every objective, at least the main approaches can be discussed and alternatives explored. For example, will the learner conduct interviews, search a database, work in the library, undertake a survey? Will primary source material be important or will published accounts be sufficient? Who should be approached first? What books are likely to be most relevant? What are the main priorities? Where should the most effort be expended? Does there need to be a fallback position? What is the best starting point for this learner at this stage of the course?

Deciding upon a practical learning strategy is central to the whole process of developing a learning contract. In fact what is achievable in terms of the contract objectives is often determined by the availability of resources. For this reason the possibilities need to be fully explored; in the case of many technical subjects even before the objectives are finalized. Alternatives will need to be negotiated if all does not go according to plan or if priorities change. Unfortunately, learners are sometimes left to themselves at this stage and so may fail to look beyond the most readily available resources, such as books on the shelf in the nearest library.

Step 4: Determine what is to be produced

Having specified the objectives and identified the basic strategies and resources, the learner should now work closely with the adviser to agree upon what is going to be assessed and what should be produced as evidence that each of the specific objectives has been achieved. This may be determined to some extent by the formal requirements of the institution or course but there will still be a need to consider the appropriateness of the evidence to the original learning objectives.

For example, if the learning contract involves the development of a specific skill in some area, how can it be demonstrated that this skill has actually been acquired? In this case some practical, observable evidence, such as a demonstration, is required rather than a piece of written work which may only indicate knowledge of the procedures involved rather than the ability to actually perform them. If this is not possible, the original objective will need to be redrafted to better reflect something that is achievable and accessible. Examples of evidence of learning that might be considered include reports and essays as well as presentations and designs and non-print media.

The important thing is that the item produced for assessment is consistent with both the type of learning involved and the expectations of the institution for the level of course being undertaken. Hence this section of the learning contract needs to be carefully considered when the learning objectives are first formulated. The length of a piece of written work, the depth of treatment expected and the number of sources to be consulted should be discussed with the adviser at this stage of the negotiations.

Personal reflection/analysis is often part of the learning process and, if so, the contract must include a reflective or analytical component. Simple descriptive or narrative accounts are not normally sufficient.

Step 5: Determine the criteria for assessment

This step, usually the most difficult part of the contract to complete, requires the learner and the adviser to agree upon appropriate quality standards for the completed work. To do this they will first have to consider the type of criteria which are most appropriate for each of the learning objectives. This will vary depending upon the nature of the objective, for example whether it is a skill or knowledge objective, and for the stage and level of the course the learner is undertaking. What may be acceptable early in a course may be inadequate later on.

Criteria for knowledge objectives will tend to be based around considerations of how comprehensive, accurate and appropriate the work is. For skill objectives, there may be a need to provide evidence of accuracy, speed and confidence. In the latter stages of a course a learner could reasonably be expected to show critical and reflective approaches to the topic under discussion or to demonstrate creative and innovative applications of a skill.

Often there are well-defined minimum criteria which apply to any work of a certain type. For example, an essay may have a specified word length, must develop an argument in a logical manner, consider alternative views and use correct procedures for referencing and constructing a bibliography. A report must be in a particular format, with sections and sub-sections and perhaps a list of recommendations. If such conventions exist, they need to be clarified at this stage. Publications which discuss style, layout and referencing should be consulted.

At times it may be desirable for the learner to obtain feedback from other people due to their particular expertise or interest in the project. This should be discussed with the adviser and thought given as to how this feedback might be incorporated into the assessment.

A further consideration is the form the assessment could take. The following questions should be considered at this stage:

- What form of self-assessment should be undertaken before submitting the completed work for formal assessment?
- Does the student require written comments or would a face-to-face discussion be preferable?
- Is an evaluative report needed?
- Does the student prefer marker's comments not to be written on the actual documents?
- Should the assessor make use of a rating scale or a checklist?
- Are indications of achievement level, such as marks, grades or merit ratings, useful or irrelevant? If they are to be used, what will be the specific criteria for each level of achievement?

Each course will have its own marking and recording conventions but there is no reason an assessment cannot be tailored to meet some particular needs of the person submitting the work for assessment. This section of the learning contract, although sometimes difficult, is nevertheless important in clarifying exactly what is expected by both parties. The benefit a learner derives from a learning activity may be related to the quality of the feedback which is received. Therefore it is desirable to specify as nearly as possible the form this feedback should take. The desire to 'validate' one's learning against some external criteria is a natural characteristic of learners in most educational settings.

Step 6: Review the learning contract

Having completed the draft of the contract proposal it is a good idea for the learner to review it a few days later to ensure it matches the original intention. It may also help to discuss it with someone else, such as a fellow student, in order to obtain a fresh perspective and to ensure commitment to what has actually been written.

While a contract is negotiated between a learner and an adviser it may not result from a single consultation. Some learners will find they wish to revise or refine parts of the original draft or even rethink their original learning objectives. With learners experienced in the use of learning contracts and those able to work independently, it is common for a full initial draft to be presented to the adviser at the start of the negotiation process.

Whatever the case, it is important to ensure each section is clear and complete and reflects the agreed activities and assessment items. Ultimately the success of the completed contract will be judged by how well it meets the stated criteria. For this reason alone all aspects of the contract proposal need to be carefully reviewed.

Step 7: Carry out the contract

The learning contract is finally signed by both the learner and the adviser and a date for completion agreed. The learner is then free to work on the project until it is ready to be submitted for assessment. The level of ongoing supervision provided by the adviser will have been discussed early in the negotiations as this will vary according to the preference and experience of the learner, the requirements of the adviser and the overall level of staff resources provided for this activity. Should the learner, in the process of conducting the learning project, wish to alter the original contract or change direction in some way this should be possible. However, the learner should always consult again with the adviser and discuss any changes which he or she may wish to make and have the adviser sign-off the changes agreed.

People's ideas about what is important or relevant often change as they become more familiar with a subject. Or they may find that while their learning objectives remain the same they have changed their ideas about how best to achieve them. This is the great strength of the learning contract method: it enables the learner to continually evaluate his or her own learning and to modify the work to suit emerging needs.

Step 8: Self-assess and submit the completed work

The first and most important person the contract must satisfy is the learner. Although learners will be making their own informal assessments throughout their learning programme about the extent to which the outcomes satisfy their original intentions, it can be useful to include a final, more formal, step before presenting their work for assessment by others. This self-assessment can take many forms. The simplest is to use the items in the agreed contract as a checklist to ensure each has been met in the way specified or otherwise adequately considered.

An alternative is to use a self-assessment schedule as a means of enabling learners to bring together a wide range of their learning in a course, to reflect on their achievements and to examine the implications for further learning. A completed schedule is a document in which learners are required to identify the objectives they have been pursuing during a course (their own and others, predetermined and emergent), establish criteria for judging the achievement of these objectives, explain what evidence they have which will demonstrate their achievements (written work, contributions to class, notes on readings, feedback from others, etc.), make judgements about the extent and quality of their achievements and report on what further action they need to engage in (if any) with respect to any of the objectives which they have set (Boud, 1992; 1995). If desired, this can act as a supplement to other products or be part of the original negotiated workplan.

The final assessment will rest with the assessor appointed by the institution or identified in the contract. This person is usually the learner's adviser for the project, but on occasions another staff member or subject expert may be used. Apart from evaluating the completed work, the assessor has a responsibility to provide feedback to the learner on both the content and presentation of the work, its overall quality and any suggestions for improvement. If contracts are not graded, this feedback becomes important in providing the learner with an indication of achievement levels.

Advisers sometimes wish to see drafts of work in progress as a means of maintaining contact with their learners and discussing any problems that may have arisen. Since most contracts are criterion-referenced, assessors may provide learners with the opportunity to resubmit incomplete work if time permits. Extensions to agreed deadlines can be arranged in accordance with institutional policy.

Developing a learning contract: A case study

In this section each of the steps involved in developing a learning contract is described using an example from a particular course. The learner, Mary Fielding, is in her first year of an undergraduate degree programme and is undertaking a course in communication. She is having her first discussion with her adviser about a learning contract for this subject.

Background

Mary has recently been to her first study group meeting for the semester. Each study group consists of six to eight students on the course who will work together on a number of set tasks during the year. The members of the group are randomly selected from the course and come from a variety of backgrounds. Mary has been elected Chair of the group. While Mary is keen on the idea of working closely with other students on a project, she is a little apprehensive about how well the group will work together. During the first meeting two or three individuals tended to dominate the discussion and some others appeared withdrawn and contributed little. Strong differences of opinion were expressed at times and at one point Mary had to intervene to stop a heated argument developing. Mary wonders if these differences may lead to problems in the future and considers requesting a move to another group.

Step 1: Establish a relevant learning need

Soon after the course starts she sees her adviser and it becomes clear that the situation in her study group is a concern for Mary. The adviser suggests that rather than move to another group, she could use the experience to develop her own competence in the area of managing conflict within a group. Mary agrees that such a skill would also be of considerable use in her future career.

As the group chair she is very aware of the need to make the study group sessions interesting and productive for all participants. At the same time she is unsure of the best approach to take when people want to dominate the discussion with their own opinions. Her adviser suggests that a slightly more assertive approach by Mary may be called for. She must ensure balanced contributions from all participants and guard against dominating the discussion herself. While discussing Mary's prior experience in other groups, Mary begins to realize there are really many aspects of group leadership she needs to learn about. At this point the adviser is able to show Mary how these issues are related to the course.

Together they work out that there are a number of specific competences which Mary would like to improve and that she will gradually tackle these over the coming months.

Step 2: Refine the learning need into specific objectives

Her adviser has established that Mary has some prior team experience to draw upon but has never before been responsible for managing a group of her peers. They agree that chairing a study group and ensuring task deadlines are met may require an understanding of group dynamics in addition to various other communication skills. Mary mentions that she has always been interested in group dynamics and wonders whether this could form the basis for a learning contract in the subject of communications. Her adviser suggests that 'group dynamics' by itself may be too broad and that in a learning contract she would be better off if she identified some particular aspect of this topic to focus on.

Mary and her adviser therefore start to pin down exactly what she will do. Since Mary's immediate concern is with conflict resolution within a small group they decide to make this the basis for her first contract. They use the course documents to identify the specific skill areas Mary will be addressing and then the learning contract form to assist in formulating the details of the contract.

First they record general information. The adviser determines the general course area the project falls into. Taking into account Mary's other commitments and the fact that there are other contracts to complete in addition to this one, Mary and her adviser set a feasible date for completion. They then decide upon the specific learning objectives. The adviser begins by asking Mary to specify her purpose in doing this project. They then identify what is needed in order for the purpose to be realized. These items become separate learning objectives for Mary. It is important that both Mary and her adviser are in agreement on these objectives before she starts work. The first part of Mary's contract form is then completed.

LEARNING CONTRACT FORM

Student: Mary Fielding

Topic/competency area: Communications – Group Leadership

Date started: 18 March

Date due for completion: 10 June

Learning Objectives

1. To identify characteristics of effective study/work groups.
2. To examine conflict resolution strategies which may be used in a group setting.
3. To critically analyse what key writers see as the skills required of a group leader.
4. To efficiently manage a group and lead a productive discussion in a situation in which potential for conflict exists.

Step 3: Identify useful resources and strategies for learning

The next step is to match suitable learning resources and strategies to these objectives. Here they discuss the most useful ways of accomplishing each objective. Mary has already given this some thought but her adviser is able to recommend some additional readings.

LEARNING RESOURCES AND STRATEGIES

1. Conduct literature search in library.
2. Read books on group dynamics and conflict resolution.
3. Read articles in journals dealing with discussion leading and small group communications.
4. Interview other study group leaders.
5. Refer to course handouts on assertive/non-assertive behaviour and group discussion.
6. Conduct a study group meeting to apply what I have discovered.

Step 4: Determine what is to be produced

Mary and her adviser then agree upon what she will produce and submit for assessment as evidence of having achieved the learning objectives. Mary feels a combination of a report and a record of an actual group session will give the best indication of her competence and understanding.

WHAT WILL BE PRODUCED

1. A written report which analyses the nature of effective work groups and discusses strategies for conflict resolution in small groups
2. An agenda plan for use in a study group meeting which incorporates opportunities for group discussion.
3. A videotaped presentation of a study group meeting in which I apply discussion leading/conflict resolution skills.

Step 5: Determine the criteria for assessment

Mary and her adviser then agree on what standard of performance is required in the things to be assessed. Here they agree on what quantity (eg, word length) is to be presented and what quality of work is expected. It is important that this section of the contract be completed to the satisfaction of both parties and that each is clear as to how the final product will be assessed.

The adviser considers such factors as the level of the course, the requirements of the institution and Mary's previous experience. The adviser also has in mind what other learners are doing or have done in the past. Mary is encouraged to think in terms of what is achievable for her and in what areas she particularly wants feedback. If the criteria are clear there should be no surprises for her in terms of the final assessment.

It is also possible for Mary to involve other people in her assessment if she considers they have specialist knowledge and could provide useful feedback. For example, she might approach colleagues with more experience in this area to sit in on one of her group's sessions. As other people are to become involved in the assessment this is recorded in this section of the contract.

ASSESSMENT CRITERIA

1. Report in standard report format, 2,500 words, correct referencing, evidence of wide reading and personal reflection. Should include a critical analysis of three major writers in the field.
2. Study group session agenda follows sound principles of planning for meetings.
3. Session to be evaluated by adviser and participants on success of the discussion, conflict management techniques employed and satisfaction of participants.

Step 6: Review the learning contract

When all sections of the contract have been completed, Mary reviews all the items to make sure they accurately reflect her real needs and interests and that the strategies she has selected are likely to be useful to her. She also looks to see if the items in the four columns are consistent with each other. She shows the contract to another lecturer she knows for additional comments and discusses the project with other students on the course, including members of the study group she intends to involve. In this way she is assured that the contract is clear and achievable and she feels confident about what she is undertaking. The contract is then signed by both Mary and her adviser and Mary begins her study.

Step 7: Carry out the contract

Mary undertakes the research and writing in a mainly self-directed manner. She occasionally seeks advice from her adviser as her work progresses and she submits an early draft for comment.

If Mary had wished to change direction slightly or rewrite her original objectives she would have sought her adviser's agreement. She was aware that she should not change the original contract without consultation, since her final assessment would be based on the agreed objectives.

Step 8: Self-assess and submit the completed work

As a final step, Mary reviews her work to determine if it meets the agreed criteria, the standards which she has set for herself and the general standards provided in the course handbook. She is satisfied to submit her work to be assessed in the manner agreed.

As the course progresses Mary becomes more experienced in the use of learning contracts and hence more confident in her ability to propose and implement a learning project. When this happens she drafts contracts by herself and presents them to her adviser for agreement. She remembers to seek her adviser's agreement to her proposals since she is aware of the difficulties experienced by one of her friends who submitted work without prior discussion with an adviser and found that it did not meet the assessment requirements of the course.

PART II

THE ELEMENTS OF A LEARNING CONTRACT

Chapter 4

Writing learning objectives

A learning contract will only be effective if the learning objectives on which it is based are meaningful for the learner and can be successfully implemented and evaluated within the time and resources available. Specifying objectives is therefore a key part of a contract and can cause the most problems if the learner is not sure where his or her needs and interests lie.

There are many different kinds of learning and the types of goals and knowledge being pursued will influence the ways in which the contract is expressed. While the illustrations given here for the sake of exposition relate to straightforward kinds of learning which can be appreciated by a non-specialist reader, the basic approach can be applied to many different forms of knowledge. Students and advisers have used contracts in all of the following ways:

- to encourage the liberal pursuit of knowledge
- to engage in instrumental and operational learning
- to build confidence through documenting achievements
- to explore self-knowledge of a humanistic kind
- to pursue self-reflection that may lead to transformative learning
- to examine ideologies and values
- to explore learning through social action.

The choice of goal and topic will be influenced by both learners' needs and the overall context of the course they are engaged in.

Topic selection

Selecting a suitable topic based on learning needs can be difficult for novice and experienced contract users alike. Deciding initially what needs to be

learnt, identifying areas of interest, matching needs with interests and selecting a topic which will be relevant, achievable and appropriate for course
assessment is not always easy. The task is complicated when the student is
unaware of what is expected within a new subject or by a new adviser or even
what areas other students are pursuing.

When the subject matter is new it is difficult for the learner to make decisions about what should be learnt and the resources required to learn it. The
learner is simply not in a position to know. Hence those new to a particular
subject may take some time before they can identify areas they wish to
explore further. In these circumstances it is unreasonable to expect a firm
contract proposal to emerge early on or that an initial idea will remain
unchanged as the course progresses. Several drafts of a contract may be
required until a proposal emerges with which the learner feels comfortable.

Research into self-directed learning outside institutional settings, such as
that of the type initiated by Alan Tough (1979), has demonstrated that learning goals change as a learning project progresses, even if it had commenced
with clear objectives in mind. Continual refinement is also a feature of many
negotiated learning contracts. Hence topic selection should not be binding
if circumstances or interests happen to change. Of course, substantial renegotiation may not always be possible. For example, contracts used for work
experience programmes or for mastery of core knowledge or skills may limit
learners' choices to ensure that broader course objectives are met. An adviser
may also decline to accept new objectives if it appears that the learner is sub-
stituting easier alternatives to the original ones for no good reason.

Exploring new areas

Learners already familiar with the field of study sometimes have trouble
identifying an area sufficiently new and interesting to justify a learning contract. This can occur when students nearing the end of their course believe
they have exhausted possibilities for new contracts. In this case the student
will need to be challenged to look beyond their immediate world or existing
conceptions of the field to consider theories, writings and research not yet
encountered. Few subjects are so well covered as to admit no possibility of
new ideas or different interpretations. In this situation a learning contract
can resemble a small research project or a piece of scholarship well suited to
an advanced student.

At times advisers may feel uncomfortable offering advice and guidance
outside their own areas of expertise. In this case the problem may need to
be discussed openly and, if appropriate, a different adviser allocated or additional advice sought. There will usually be some teachers, librarians or external subject matter experts who can point students in the right direction and
provide assistance to draft a useful contract. Similarly, outside comment may
be requested when the final work is to be assessed. If third parties are to be

involved in either drafting or assessing the contract, their role needs to be carefully agreed at the initial negotiation stage. However, experience has shown that students are usually prepared to receive feedback from their adviser as a 'critical reader' even if this person is not the best to judge the technical content. At the undergraduate level, however, it would be unusual for a course adviser to have no knowledge of the particular subject area in which a contract was being developed.

Clarifying learner expectations

One other issue which should be considered at the topic selection stage is the likelihood of the plan being implemented. Learners are normally very enthusiastic when they first embark on an activity they have chosen, but in their enthusiasm they overestimate what they can accomplish in the time available. An unrealistic or unmanageable learning contract will create much stress and frustration later on. Advisers should ensure the learner fully understands what the proposal involves and the skills needed to accomplish it before agreement.

The opposite situation, where a learner proposes a very narrow or simplistic contract, or a contract in an area already well covered, may also arise. Here a decision needs to be made as to whether the contract represents worthwhile new learning or will assist in further development of the learner. This is an individual matter which may require detailed discussion to uncover expectations and motives. It is important that over the duration of a course both learners and advisers are satisfied that topic or competency coverage is adequate and the work attempted appropriate for the level of the course and comparable with that undertaken by others in the same programme.

Teachers need to make explicit what areas a particular course or subject covers so that thinking about possible contract topics can begin as soon as possible. Sometimes it may be useful to divide a course into three or four sections or modules and require learners to complete a separate contract for each. This can ensure coverage of key areas within the course. Alternatively a series of smaller contracts may be based on particular aspects of course content.

Finally, in selecting a topic learners should be warned against rushing in to something which they have to substantially redesign later. The opportunity to renegotiate a contract should not be used as an excuse to avoid careful initial planning. Learners need to be encouraged to read widely and to talk to others. By taking time to select a worthwhile topic they benefit more from available course materials, selected readings and discussions with their advisers.

Specifying objectives

The next step involves turning a general topic area or perceived learning need into learning objectives or statements of intended learning outcomes. The requirement to formulate specific learning objectives prior to the commencement of a learning activity is a common cause for concern. Having a desire to explore a certain topic area does not necessarily enable a learner to specify what it is that will be learnt.

For example, it is not possible to predict precisely where new learning will lead or what the final outcome is likely to be. Interests may change or develop in different directions once learning has commenced. If learning is seen as a journey with value for its own sake, rather than as a means to an end, there can be philosophical objections to anticipating precise outcomes. In such cases, thinking in terms of a more general learning aim or goal may be a useful intermediate step. In many circumstances advisers should be prepared to accept less specific statements of intent so long as the final product submitted for assessment is appropriate for the course. However, regardless of the form the objective takes, it should still be constructed in such a way as to give a clear sense of direction.

Behavioural and non-behavioural objectives

The strong influence of behavioural objectives in earlier years has led many people to assume that the objectives of a learning contract should be expressed in behavioural or operational terms: that is, they should begin with an action verb and be specific, observable and measurable. Such a requirement is unnecessary. The rigorous application of behavioural objectives can be far too limiting if contracts are to reflect a genuine learning process. It is certainly possible to have a goal in mind, based upon the reason for undertaking the learning in the first place, but this goal may be as broad or as narrow as one wishes.

A desire to learn more about a particular subject or to improve one's understanding of a certain issue can be a legitimate objective. Indeed, this degree of generality is frequently quite appropriate when initially developing a learning contract. Other parts of the contract can be used to clarify or define the general learning objective if there is a need to do so. Discussions between the student and the adviser will determine the level of specificity required for a particular course or topic.

On some occasions it may not be possible to be precise about learning objectives, resources to be used nor final assessment criteria. In such cases it is worth remembering that a learning contract is essentially a tool to assist the learner. Provided the contract remains relevant to the needs of both the learner and the formal requirements of the course, subsequent refinements of an earlier draft may be possible. Learners who spend too long agonizing over the wording of objectives are placing an unnecessary burden upon themselves at a time when their energies would be better spent getting started. More exact wordings can usually be supplied once the project gets underway.

Of course this is not to suggest behavioural objectives should be avoided altogether. If the agreed objectives are clear and precise at the outset it will certainly make subsequent planning and assessment that much easier. Some learning contracts will have a very specific focus and in such cases more precise objectives are required. For example, contracts developed in technical or skill areas may aim to show the exact type of information or skill the learner seeks to acquire. An objective such as 'to learn more about electric circuits' obviously does not communicate intention as well as one that specifies what is to be learnt. In this instance 'to calculate the resistance in various circuits by applying Ohm's law' gives a much clearer picture of what the student should focus on. This is closer to a behavioural objective since it specifies a type of outcome – mathematical calculation – which can be demonstrated by the learner and observed by the assessor. But while such objectives provide a definite focus and limit the range of the contract, there will still be times when a high degree of specificity is not possible nor desirable. For example, 'to increase my understanding of the ethical values involved in patient care' may be more appropriate in many situations than an objective that seeks to limit or enumerate these values. Whatever the case, students need to know what kinds of objective are acceptable to advisers. (For a fuller discussion of this issue see Brookfield, 1986.)

The objectives define the learning intention. Since the contract will be assessed to a large extent on how well it meets its own objectives it is important to make these objectives as meaningful as possible. This will depend on both the nature of the topic area and the expectations advisers have for learners undertaking the course concerned. Time spent clarifying learning goals and objectives will make the subsequent parts of the contract that much easier to develop.

Chapter 5

Identifying resources and strategies for learning

Developing a learning contract requires not only awareness of the objectives and likely outcomes of the learning process but, equally as important, consideration of how each learning objective will be achieved.

Despite the fact that a contract is a device used to facilitate the learning *process*, many learners tend to gloss over the column that asks them to identify 'Resources and strategies'. They often fail to think beyond books and journals on reading lists. Yet this section of the contract is most important. If the proposed objectives are to be met, and the learning process made easier and more rewarding, a viable 'action plan' must first be developed and a diverse list of useful resources drawn up. The adviser is crucial at this stage since learners may not be aware of the resources available to them or of alternative approaches which may prove useful.

Learning resources

Most students think of books when considering likely resources, yet books are only one (and not always the best) type of resource. Even in traditional academic courses, much learning occurs in ways which have little to do with published works. This is not to diminish the importance of books but rather to encourage learners to think more widely and more imaginatively when identifying the means to meet their learning needs.

A richer and more complete learning outcome is perhaps more likely if a range of resources can be consulted. Anything which may be able to add to knowledge, understanding or skills is a potential resource. Any person who knows something learners want to find out about is also a resource. Any method for accessing these people and materials is a potential learning strategy.

Students use a diversity of resources and strategies at different times. Below is a list of resources students claimed to have consulted during the preparation of their learning contracts (Sampson *et al.*, 1992).

RESOURCES USED BY STUDENTS

- Books and journals
- Other written materials
  – newspapers, magazines,
  brochures, manuals, newsletters,
  conference papers, pamphlets
- Government or other
  official publications and
  documents
- Course handouts and
  lecture notes
- CD Roms, e-mail and other
  electronic media
- Case notes
- Films and video tapes
- Television and radio
  programmes
- Audio cassettes
- Networks of peers,
  fellow students

- Subject-matter experts
- University teaching staff
- Librarians
- Work colleagues
- Supervisors and
  managers
- Family and friends
- Seminars and
  conferences
- Course workshops
- Notes from other
  courses
- Field visits, excursions
- Personal diary or journal
- Resource centres
- Trade unions
- Professional associations

Ethical issues

An important part of the adviser's role is that of advising learners of ethical considerations in connection with their proposed learning activities. Most institutions have formal ethics policies which can be consulted. While these generally pertain to research projects, learning contracts sometimes include a research component such as a questionnaire or a series of personal interviews. Less experienced students need to be advised of the potential pitfalls of these methods and all should be provided with information about the institution's policy (for example, concerning the use of humans in research, confidentiality issues, etc). Legal and moral responsibilities must be considered when dealing with other people and a plea of ignorance is not usually acceptable as an excuse. When planning an approach to learning or when thinking about ways of obtaining information ethical issues arise and the adviser should be expected to have a part to play both in helping learners think these through and in having a position to represent.

Personal resources

For all students, the ability to identify and evaluate the range of methods and materials available to them will increase as they become more familiar with their field of study. A willingness to actively seek out sources of ideas and information and explore different techniques for learning is essential for learners to gain maximum benefit from working with learning contracts.

At this point the main role of the staff adviser is to establish an environment which will support and promote learning. This naturally includes advice regarding books, materials and learning strategies but the level of support may also go beyond this. Many students are anxious about the whole process and negative feelings need to be dealt with in an honest and open manner if a productive learning relationship with the adviser is to develop. Chapter 12 suggests ways in which an adviser can assist learners throughout the process.

The adviser can become one of the learner's most important personal resources. By being available to offer advice and support, in addition to clarifying academic and assessment issues, the adviser can do much to ensure the learning process is as fruitful as possible.

Also important is the network of friends and colleagues the learner can draw upon. These people can be helpful in many respects. For instance, initial ideas for a learning contract may come from fellow students or work colleagues. As the project gets underway, encouragement, feedback and advice can be sought from those who have a close personal or professional relationship with the student. Often friends, work colleagues and fellow students are also valuable sources of factual information and by sharing their knowledge and experience make the learning task that much easier for someone encountering a topic area for the first time. People and their diverse skills can be a resource for virtually any learning contract. For this reason the use of peer support strategies, such as learning partners or organized study groups, is highly recommended (see Chapter 12).

Learning strategies

Developing a learning strategy involves identifying sources of information and determining suitable methods for accessing them. For instance, if published material is to be consulted, how current or context-specific does it need to be? If certain people are to be approached should this be done in writing, perhaps by means of a questionnaire, or in person? How formal should any interviews be? How can data obtained be verified? Are there any less obvious sources which might provide useful ideas, perspectives or interpretations? These types of consideration require learners to think carefully and proactively about their intentions. They require a degree of investigative skill which extends beyond the common practice of simply browsing along a library shelf in the hope that a relevant title may appear. The learning styles and preferences of the learner are also important to consider at this stage.

Determining appropriate resources and strategies is a basic investigative skill. In the case of preparing a learning contract emphasis is on those resources most likely to contain material relevant to the specific objectives of the contract. In one sense almost anything, from a television programme to a casual conversation, can be a resource for learning. The task is to decide which resources are most suitable to meet each of the learning objectives. Often it is difficult to determine this in advance. Identifying resources is part of the learning process, as one item frequently leads to a new and previously unknown source.

Since knowledge of resources will increase the more that is known about the topic area, the 'Resources and strategies' section of the learning contract, like other sections, should not be regarded as final and unchangeable. It is there to provide a starting point and a map to guide the process. Yet like all maps, the more salient detail it provides the more useful it will prove to be. Discussions between the student and the adviser will enable a start to be made, while a wider range of resources will no doubt be uncovered as the project continues.

Chapter 6

Deciding what will be produced

What will result as evidence of a successful learning outcome depends upon the objectives being pursued by the learner and the assessment criteria which must be met. The choice of work and the form it takes must reflect these. The final product should adequately portray what has been achieved. In most situations students elect to produce written work as evidence that their learning objectives have been met. The essay or formal report are by far the most common types of product resulting from the completion of a learning contract.

However, many other options are available, depending upon the kind of learning outcomes the learner is seeking. One popular alternative with small groups of students is the class presentation. This involves individuals or groups reporting to the others the results of their learning projects. The use of such group activities helps make learning something which is shared and contributes to the learning of others. The resources used to make such a presentation then become a part of the learning contract. In other cases, the results of the project may be reported in graphic or electronic forms as suitable for the area under study.

In a performance-based contract, such as those negotiated as part of a work experience programme, other possible options could include a skill demonstration, procedural notes, clinical or case notes, a critical incident log or even an oral examination. A reflective diary or journal is often used in conjunction with other assessment items to encourage learners to adopt a more analytical and reflective approach to their experiences.

The following list suggests the range of materials which can be produced to indicate the achievement of the contract's objectives.

TYPES OF COMPLETED EVIDENCE

- Annotated bibliography
- Artwork, graphic design
- Audio-visual presentation
- Booklet
- Book review
- Business plan
- Business report
- Case studies
- Class presentation
- Clinical notes
- Commentaries
- Conference paper
- Computer software
- Demonstration
- Designs, blueprints
- Diagrams
- Diary or personal journal
- Discussion leader's guide
- Essay
- Evaluation report
- Film or video review
- Guidebook
- Interview transcripts
- Job aids
- Job-related materials
- Journal paper
- Laboratory report
- Management report
- Mind maps or concept maps
- Minutes of meetings
- Newspaper and magazine articles
- Personal reflections
- Photographs and slides
- Posters
- Procedural manual
- Project plan
- Recorded interview
- Research report
- Resource kit
- Solutions to problems
- Training manual
- Trainer's notes
- Video presentation
- Work experience report.

Linking evidence of outcomes with goals

Whatever form they take, the items selected as evidence should be the most appropriate means of demonstrating that the aims and objectives of the learning contract have been met. For instance, a formal essay provides good evidence of the achievement of some kinds of academic objectives, such as critical appraisal, but is an inappropriate way of demonstrating others, such as the mastery of a new mechanical skill. Consideration needs to be given to the relationship between the learning goals and the type of evidence which would be most suitable. The following table gives examples of types of objectives and how they might be linked with appropriate forms of evidence.

Type of goal/objective	Possible types of evidence
Skill	Demonstration (live or video-taped).
Knowledge	Essay, report, annotated bibliography, oral presentation, audio-visual presentation.
Understanding	Essay, evaluation report, case study, research report, concept map, project plan.
Problem solving	Examples of problems and solutions, strategies for approaching problems.
Attitudes	Rating scales, simulation exercises, role plays, critical incident case studies, discussion.
Communication skills	Examples in medium in which communication is being developed, eg video or audio tape, business report, oral presentation, letters, articles.
Conceptual development	Models, diagrams, concept maps, case studies with commentaries.
Design skills	Examples of product, artwork, blueprints, models, account of process steps.
Critical reflection	Personal journals or journal overviews, records of debriefing sessions, transcripts of peer discussions, book reviews, analysis of issues.
Work-related competences	Business plan, project management plan, management reports, budgets, records.

There are instances when no decisions need to be made regarding what to produce. There are quite often accepted ways in which a learner is assessed or a skill demonstrated. For example, in many subjects the critical essay is the main means of presenting the results of one's reading, thinking and analysis. Writing such an essay becomes a skill in itself, part of initiation into the discipline, and is the standard form in which ideas are communicated. If the learning contract is designed to help plan a series of practical learning activities, as is the case with field experience programmes, the mode of assessment is usually determined by the nature of the activity itself. For instance, correctly reading a patient's blood pressure or preparing a patient for minor surgery are nursing skills best demonstrated through performance.

In other cases there may be considerable scope for original, often creative, products. A psychology student wishing to obtain feedback on counselling skills may choose to submit a recorded interview (video or audio) of an actual or simulated counselling session; an architecture student may supplement a theoretical essay on future design trends with personal illustrations or plans based upon an imaginary scenario; a trainee teacher may present materials produced for a class and explain the ideas underlying the selection.

Assessment or learning?

In such cases a distinction needs to be made between whether the product is a means of providing evidence of learning or whether in fact the product is part of the learning itself. While there is always an element of learning contained within any assessment, a video designed to record a counselling session will be judged quite differently depending upon whether the contract is concerned with learning video production skills or counselling skills. Similarly, an audio tape intended to be used for relaxation or motivational purposes is a very different product to one which is simply a record of a conversation. Some students may choose to submit personal reflections or critiques on tape rather than in written form or to create a finished piece of art or design. The degree to which the content and the presentation combine, and the emphasis placed upon each in the final assessment, is a matter for careful negotiation.

While the possibilities seem endless, in reality the product will tend to be limited by considerations such as the nature of the course in which the contract is developed, the preferences of the adviser and the norms established over time by other students. A student proposing a very different outcome needs to assure the adviser that the work envisaged is comparable, in terms of effort and difficulty, with the work being undertaken by others in the course. It would then be up to the adviser to determine parity between different types of contracts.

Chapter 7

Determining assessment criteria

The purpose of assessment is essentially twofold: to provide feedback to learners and to indicate to learners and others a standard of achievement. In a totally self-directed situation this latter purpose is not often relevant as the satisfaction of the learner with the completed learning is sufficient. In a university or other educational setting, however, assessment becomes a major issue, particularly when independent learning contracts are undertaken. There is an implicit acknowledgment when signing a contract that students agree to non-negotiable components of assessment. This point is important, since these components are not normally written into the contract itself.

A learning contract can be used as *part* of an assessment strategy rather than as the sole means of assessment. In this case, when negotiating contracts advisers can take account of what other types of assessment are employed and the demands likely to be placed on students. For instance, a contract may be particularly suitable for an extended discussion or in-depth analysis of particular issues if the other type of assessment is a multiple-choice test. Whatever the case, there should be no suggestion that because students undertaking contracts have more freedom to select their topics and approaches that the final product is in any way inferior to a traditional assignment. The opposite is frequently the case, with students making greater effort and producing far more than they otherwise might. Adviser expectations and assessment requirements need to be made clear early in the process. It is also important for the general acceptance of the learning contract method that assessment criteria are public and visible.

Deciding how much is required

A question which learners frequently ask is, 'How long should the completed work be?' There is obviously no simple answer to this question. Yet the reply,

'As long as it needs to be' will usually be greeted with confusion or dismay. For this reason word or time requirements are often built into the contract as part of the assessment criteria and these should be consistent for all students undertaking the course. These figures can be derived from consideration of what is required in other subjects at the same level or, where they exist, from policy statements connecting the number of credit points gained from completing a particular activity with the number of notional student study hours involved.

A variation on this institutionally-driven response is to offer learners the opportunity to negotiate several contracts of different length based upon their own perceived learning needs. The adviser's aim is to ensure parity between learners in such cases. Another option, more in keeping with the original philosophy of contracts, is for learners to progress at their own pace until they are satisfied with the outcome, regardless of word length or time taken. This encourages more enthusiastic learners to achieve a lot from the contract without frustrating or penalizing others.

When students can demonstrate their work in a variety of forms, there needs to be some way of ensuring that there is a balance of educational effort across different media and different modes of presentation. One way of dealing with this is to discuss what is to be produced in terms of *word equivalence*. Caution needs to be exercised in using time spent in production or time needed to develop new production skills as criteria. If the learning of new media skills is part of the contract then this can be considered. However, the major consideration in determining word equivalence is what is required to demonstrate the educational outcomes of the contract. The simplistic adoption of word-length or time-spent guidelines may lead students to believe that it is volume, rather than achievement, which counts. Helping students distinguish between effort and achievement is an important task for advisers.

Are some standards 'given'?

While there will usually be common requirements, the specific criteria that might be used in assessing an individual learning contract should normally be negotiated between student and adviser. However, learning contract negotiations may in fact be built upon a set of assumptions which have been taken for granted and which do not become explicit to the student until the first contract is assessed. Some of the criteria used to judge the contract are simply regarded as 'given' for any work undertaken in that course and hence not actually spelt out at the negotiation stage. These types of 'given' criteria will depend upon such factors as:

- the level of the course;
- the stage of the course (eg, first or last year);

- the size or scope of the contract (eg, a minor or major piece of work);
- the espoused standards sought by staff;
- the components that make up the contract (oral, written, other).

Expectations will vary for each of these factors and should be clarified with learners at the outset. This is particularly important for students new to the course or those who have not worked with learning contracts before. The use of learning contracts provides a challenge to staff to spell out criteria which previously have remained unstated.

Selecting assessment criteria

After considering the expectations and assumptions which underpin the final assessment, advisers can assist learners by placing contractual expectations within a framework of overall course requirements. This could be done by identifying areas of knowledge or competency still to be covered and topics which could be addressed in future contracts. It may also be useful for each student to consider which of the assessment criteria need to be used to provide evidence of learning. Ways of assessing each could be discussed and thought given to the type of feedback preferred. There may even be the option to involve other parties, such as an employer or fellow students, in the assessment process. Questions such as the following are often helpful for students in determining how the finished contract might be judged.

QUESTIONS TO HELP STUDENTS JUDGE
FINISHED WORK

1. *At the personal level*
   - On reflection, what do I now know or understand that I didn't before?
   - Has this work met my original learning needs?
   - How does the work illustrate what new knowledge I have gained?
   - Have I questioned my original ideas and assumptions?
   - Is this the learning that I wanted to do and of my own choice?

2. *At the task level*
   - Is the work presented adequate for the purpose?
   - Is there an overall coherence in the work?

- Is the work free of errors in spelling, grammar, punctuation, style, etc?
- Is there sufficient evidence of wider (appropriate) reading?
- Is there consistency in voice (personal or impersonal) and tense?
- Have correct referencing procedures been used?
- Are the conclusions supported by argument and/or evidence?
- Is there evidence of original ideas or interpretations?

3. *At the impact level*
   - Has it helped me in my work or with my understanding of this subject?
   - Has it assisted my personal development?
   - Has this learning had any effect on other people I deal with?
   - Has the theory made a difference to how I work or plan to work in the future?
   - Has this learning changed me in my workplace or as a student on this course?
   - Overall, has the result justified the effort?

While such questions may be part of the informal self-assessment that learners undertake prior to submitting their final work for marking, to pose them in such a formal way could be seen as yet another strange and demanding part of the learning contract process. Advisers may therefore prefer to wait until learners are more comfortable with the whole business of negotiation before introducing these questions.

Criteria used by assessors

A survey of academic staff who have used the learning contract method over a number of years provided some clear indications of the types of things they expected in a completed learning contract (see Anderson *et al.*, 1992). Staff were asked to nominate the main qualities they looked for in a contract submitted for assessment and what they considered were the minimum, non-negotiable requirements for a satisfactory contract. The responses to this survey, clarified through subsequent discussions and meetings, suggest the following are important when assessing contracts.

GENERAL FACTORS IN ASSESSMENT OF CONTRACTS

- Achievement of the contract objectives.
- Quality of presentation (this includes completeness, layout, structure and organization, clarity of expression, correct referencing procedures).
- Critical reflection and original thought.
- Evidence of further reading and research.
- An attempt to link theory and practice.
- Evidence of new learning.
- A logical argument or an awareness of the key issues relevant to a topic area.
- The usefulness of the project to the learner.
- The satisfaction of the learner with the completed work.

Other criteria may apply to particular types of contracts or in particular practice-oriented courses. For example:

- transcripts of interviews edited in ways which do not distort the point of view of those interviewed;
- work study or case notes recorded accurately and sighted by the field supervisor;
- implications for practice and the student's own work;
- extent of change in the student's workplace or work-related activities resulting from the contract.

In summary, in determining assessment criteria there is a need to consider both the process and the product. The learner should be encouraged to think beyond simply producing an item for final assessment. The contract should be seen as a developmental activity wherein the learning experience itself is recognized and valued and the outcomes judged with respect to the standards which apply to authentic work of the type produced. At the original negotiation stage, decisions must be made as to how best to demonstrate the quality of what has been learnt.

What is not negotiable?

Learning contracts provide considerable freedom for learners to select and design learning experiences relevant to their own needs and interests. Yet their use as a vehicle for accreditation naturally imposes limitations upon this freedom. Any learning contract will have non-negotiable components. These are typically related to matters about which there exists a departmental policy or about which staff hold strong value positions. Often these are implied rather than stated and the learning contract assumes an agreement to these on the part of the student. It is not desirable for these to remain implicit since students may rightly object to not knowing the factors influencing their assessment.

In the context of a learning contract negotiated within an institutional setting, the following are examples of matters usually considered not negotiable:

- The learning plan, in the form of a written contract, must be formally approved by an adviser prior to the completion of the learning activities.
- The contract proposal must fall within the bounds of the subject and be consistent with the objectives or competences of the subject in which the student is enrolled. In the case of individualized projects which cross subject boundaries, the proposal must be consistent with the overall goals of the course.
- For students currently employed, the work presented cannot be solely that produced for a work assignment in their organization. However, such work may form a major part of a contract if agreed by the adviser so long as there is documented evidence of additional subject/course related learning. (This requirement may be varied depending upon how much academic credit is granted for actual work achievements.)
- The completed work must be presented using inclusive (eg, non-sexist) language.
- The level of achievement to be demonstrated (in, for example, writing, analysis and skill of performance) must be consistent with the level of course and the stage of the course reached by the student.
- Final work must be submitted by the announced or negotiated deadlines.

Non-negotiable academic criteria

The following are normally regarded as non-negotiable features and the interpretation of them would vary according to the level of the course. However, in the case of a sequence of contracts it may not be necessary that each contract meets all the requirements if the sequence of contracts taken together does so.

**GENERAL NON-NEGOTIABLE ASSESSMENT CRITERIA
FOR ACADEMIC WORK**

- Evidence of analysis and critical thinking
- Use of multiple sources
- Reference to appropriate literature
- Use of argument supported by evidence
- Some element of personal reflection
- Logical development and structure.

When a learner produces a draft learning contract proposal the adviser may recommend modifications. In particular the adviser must reserve the right to establish assessment criteria and deadlines for final submission. It is at this point that expectations are clarified and an agreement made as to the form and quality standards of the completed work. It is important that students are aware of what is and what is not negotiable. While it can be useful to have lists of non-negotiable criteria of the kind discussed above, there are dangers that students may perceive a set of requirements as excessively narrowing options before they have considered their own criteria. The adviser has an important role in drawing attention to the considerable range of choices of assessment criteria which are still possible within the 'givens'.

As learners become more familiar with drafting contracts and receiving feedback, issues of assessment become less problematic. An advantage of the learning contract method is that, if the process has been carefully followed, the final assessment should hold neither threat nor surprise.

An example of assessment criteria

The following example is taken from a handbook for physiotherapy students at the University of East London and illustrates how appropriate assessment criteria can be developed along with learning objectives for various components of a clinical education programme.

What do I want to learn?	By what standards will my performance be judged?
Problem solving To carry out an appropriate respiratory assessment.	Complete, uses all sources, logical examination, uses time well, accurately identifies patient's problems, goals linked to pathology/patient lifestyle, justifies treatment, knows when to modify treatment.
Treatment management To apply a range of techniques for peripheral joint dysfunction	Correct, fluent, accurate, good position of patient and self, responsive to patient, feels confident.
Communication To communicate effectively with variety of patients, particularly the elderly client group.	Listens, explains, instructs, gives encouragement, alters language to suit patient, uses non-verbal skills, interacts with patient.
Documentation To record the care episode.	Legible writing, uses all aspects of POR (problem-oriented record), dated, signed, accurate, consistent style.
Professional behaviour To work within the team and to be perceived as a 'physiotherapist'.	Feels comfortable, tidy, punctual, maintains confidentiality, respects patient's dignity, interacts with colleagues.

Chapter 8

Examples of learning contracts

As a learning contract is a tool for planning learning, the exact form it takes will depend upon a number of factors, such as:

- the type of course in which it is being developed
- the stage or section of the course being undertaken
- the nature of the learning goals/objectives
- the type of outcomes expected
- the preferences of the learner
- the preferences of the adviser
- the formal requirements of the course or institution.

While the basic learning contract discussed so far contains the four column headings (Learning objectives, Learning resources and strategies, Evidence, and Assessment criteria), the wording of each or the number of headings may be varied to better assist learners plan for a particular course or type of learning activity. Similarly, the layout and design of the contract may vary to incorporate such features as the adviser's comments, learner notes and dates and times for completion or review. However, to ensure consistency and parity it is important to use the same form of contract for all learners undertaking a particular course or module. Once a suitable format has been decided upon all learners and advisers should follow it precisely. If changes later need to be made, these should be implemented for all learners.

On the following pages are some examples of learning contracts developed for particular courses and of contract forms used in connection with field experience programmes. Some of the variations which they illustrate will be discussed in more detail in Chapter 14. They are included here to demonstrate the diversity of forms which are used. Like all examples of negotiated learning, they would necessarily differ if there were different parties involved.

T000068

Example 1. A typical learning contract for a subject or module

This is a typical contract based upon the four standard column headings. Student and course information is completed before the actual contract details and both student and adviser sign the completed contract and retain a copy. This form of contract, while using the standard headings, reads vertically down the page rather than across. While this may make it easier to store or reproduce, it does have the disadvantage of separating the learning objectives from the other sections, making cross-referencing more difficult.

DEPARTMENT OF ADULT EDUCATION
LEARNING CONTRACT FORM

Student: Eliza Fraser
Topic/Competency: Adult Teaching and Learning
Date started: 19 March **Date due for completion:** 4 June

Learning objectives
1. To analyse the role of a training group facilitator.
2. To develop my ability to use different strategies when facilitating small group exercises and discussions.
3. To identify a model of experiential learning for use in a management training session.

Learning resources and strategies
1. Conduct literature search in library using relevant database.
2. Interview trainers and fellow students who have conducted sessions using experiential techniques.
3. Refer to course handouts on discussion leading.
4. Design and conduct a training session using an experiential exercise.

Outcomes
1. A written report which analyses the nature of group facilitation, discussion leading and experiential learning.
2. A session plan for use in management training which incorporates an experiential exercise and a facilitator's guide to debriefing.
3. A 30-minute training session presented to the tutorial class.

Assessment criteria
1. Report in standard report format, 3,000 words, correct referencing, evidence of wide reading and personal reflection. Should include a critical analysis of at least one model of experiential learning.
2. Training session follows model and is relevant to course objectives.
3. Session to be evaluated by adviser on learning outcomes, interest levels and my skills in facilitation/discussion leading.

Signature (Student) _____ Date: _____

Signature (Adviser) _____ Date: _____

Example 2. A standard learning contract with adviser's comments recorded

This is another standard contract using the four-column format. In this case the contract is required to address particular course competences. It combines knowledge objectives with a practical objective to be implemented outside the course. For this reason the student may wish to consider obtaining feedback from a manager at work in addition to assessment by the course adviser. This feedback could be taken into account when assessing the final report. The contract form also allows space for the adviser's comments, a useful feature if negotiation occurs mainly by post or fax.

Student: Terry Smith   **Course:** Bachelor of Business
Advisor: C Lee
Competencies: Performance Appraisal, Human Resource Management
Date project commenced: 10 September
Date due for completion: 12 December

Objectives	Strategies and resources	What to assess	How to assess (criteria)
1. To create a performance appraisal form for use in the workplace	Read resource material by: M Samuelson J Saville L Field D Laird Luthans and Hodgetts	1. Written report of 3,000 words	Coverage of topic
2. To understand the role of leadership in the performance appraisal process	Conduct library search of HRM journals	2. Appraisal sheets produced for use in a workplace	Adequacy of description of the appraisal process and benefits Suitability of the appraisal for the workplace
3. To explore the benefits of a staff appraisal system	Contact organizations to discuss appraisal systems		Evidence of own ideas and further reading
4. To ascertain the different methods of conducting staff appraisals			

Signature (Student): _____

Adviser's comments:

Approved: Yes/No _____ Date: _____

Signature (Adviser): _____

Example 3. A competency-based learning contract

This contract was developed by a student in computing science and illustrates how a learning contract may be used in a purely technical subject, in this case database. The objectives are based upon the learning interests of the student at the time the contract was developed and learning occurs in a mainly self-directed manner, although course lectures are identified as a learning resource. There is a competency-based approach to assessment and the contract forms part of the overall assessment for this particular subject.

LEARNING CONTRACT PROPOSAL FORM

Student: N Mospas   **Subject:** Database
Adviser: S Chardsonick
Date agreed: **Date due:**

Learning objectives	Strategies and resources	What is to be assessed	Criteria for assessment
1. Learn SQL syntax	Textbooks to gain understanding of statement structure	1. Computer print-outs showing SQL statements and results of problems	Effectiveness and efficiency of SQL solutions to set of problems
2. Discover how to structure queries to execute efficiently	Manuals to help understand syntax and analyse errors	2. Written explanations of reasons for using particular approaches to solving problems	Understanding exhibited by reasoning behind approach to solutions
3. Solve the attached set of problems using SQL	Online help and tutorials Expert input from academic staff		Competence in using manuals

Signature (Student): _____

Contact Nos (Student)   Tel: _____ Fax: _____

Signature (Advisor): _____

Contact Nos (Staff)   Tel: _____ Fax: _____

Example 4. Graded contract for a clinical experience programme

This contract was developed for the clinical placement component of a course in physiotherapy and includes a variety of learning goals. The goals are determined by the student early in the placement and discussed with the clinical supervisor and university tutor. The tutor decides if the goals are appropriate for the student concerned and the stage of the course which has been reached, while the clinical supervisor discusses what resources and opportunities are available to address each goal. The supervisor also discusses with the student the most appropriate means of assessment for each (test, observation, patient feedback, peer review, etc).

Two interesting points about this particular version are that the written contract is not compulsory if a student prefers a more directed placement and that the contract is undertaken in conjunction with a personal diary in which experiences and feelings are recorded to discuss with the supervisor at regular times during the placement.

QUEEN ELIZABETH SCHOOL OF PHYSIOTHERAPY
LEARNING CONTRACT

Negotiated between: 1. Sue Knowles (Student)
Location: Hope Hospital (neurological in-patients)

2. Janet Ferrier (Facilitator)
Target date for completion: 7 February

Goals	Strategies and resources	Criteria and means of evaluation
1. To carry out accurate gait analysis as part of patients' initial assessment in a reasonable time	*Strategies* JF to allocate a patient with gait problems to SK and a fellow student to work on together. Each student to take turns in leading the gait re-ed and feedback to the other.	*Goals 1–3* I will select a patient and give a short presentation to my fellow students and Janet, based on a video recording of his/her initial gait assessment, followed by an analysis of his progress from then on. The group will evaluate my performance according to the following criteria:-
2. To carry out progressive gait analysis throughout patients treatment programme.	SK to talk through her POMR entries with JF twice/week.	*Code Criteria* A All relevant aspects covered and conclusions accurate. B All relevant aspects covered but conclusions not completely accurate. C Analysis incomplete but those conclusions reached are accurate.
3. To present findings relating to (1) and (2) succinctly and accurately, both verbally and in written form.	SK to make at least 2 unsolicited contributions in every clinical tutorial.	D Analysis incomplete and conclusions not completely accurate. E Analysis limited and conclusions inaccurate.
4. To be confident enough to contribute equally with other students during clinical tutorials.	*Resources* Staff and their patients Peers Dept video library Practical Anatomy notes Library Communication skills, Assertiveness skills, Neuro. Theory & Practice.	Janet will evaluate my POMR (problem-oriented medical record) entries on gait using the same *Goal 4* I will reflect on my diary with Janet and try to formulate an Action Theory that I can put into practice in other situations.

Example 5. Learning contract for an industrial experience programme

The layout and section headings have been varied in this contract to place equal emphasis on each objective and to incorporate three quite different types of objectives and assessments into the one contract. The contract has been developed as part of a work experience programme and hence involves workplace personnel in the assessment, although the final objective is most appropriately assessed by the industrial experience adviser from the university. With this type of contract it is also possible to specify different completion times for each objective.

MY AIM

To understand the role of technology in engineering practice

Objective A	Objective B	Objective C
To be aware of the development of the soldering iron and be able to use it competently	To consider the impact of CAD on engineering practice in my workplace	To broaden my understanding of engineering by reading a book on engineering
Activities	**Activities**	**Activities**
Read about the history of the development of the soldering iron and how it works	Develop interview sheet	Read the 'Existential Pleasures of Engineering' by S C Florman
	Interview employees	
Practice using the soldering iron	Find out the procedures used before CAD was introduced and discuss the difference CAD has made to their work	
Evidence	**Evidence**	**Evidence**
Two-page summary of the technical development of soldering	Interview sheet	Write a four-page critique
	Collate information received into summar of interview topics	
Solder components, specified by a technical officer at work, to a breadboard	Analyse information received	
	Three-page report	
Time to complete: 9 weeks	**Time to complete:** 9 weeks	**Time to complete:** 4 weeks
Criteria for assessment	**Criteria for assessment**	**Criteria for assessment**
Completeness of summary – are all technical, aspects covered?	Quality of interview sheet – did it cover all possible issues?	How well the critique reflects knowledge and understanding of the book
Quality of solder	Analysis of findings and justification of conclusion	
Assessor	**Assessor**	**Assessor**
Technical officer at work	Work supervisor	IE adviser

Student: _____

IE Adviser: _____

Example 6. Career planning via a learning contract

This student is an engineering cadet undertaking part-time study in conjunction with work experience. The contract is unusual insofar as it involves long time spans and describes ongoing activities as well as specific learning objectives. This type of career-based learning plan can be useful at the start of a course to provide a focus and direction for study and to motivate the learner towards achieving long-term goals. Specific learning contracts for other more immediate components of the training can be used in conjunction with this plan.

LEARNING CONTRACT

Between
Jan Tiffy and Qantas Airways Limited

Objectives	Description	Achievement indicator	Time span
Mechanical engineering section	Participate in activities within the engineering office area. These activities should be relevant to university theory	Successful completion of allotted tasks	2 years
Workplace study	Complete a time management study of practices within an area of E&M. The associated report will include recommendations to the company	Completion of the task, together with an oral and written submission to the company	4 years
Annual budget	Assist in preparing the annual budget for E&M. The task will include all facets of the budget, ie analysis of previous years, forecasts and presentation	Presentation of the budget to senior management	5 years

LONG-TERM GOALS AND OBJECTIVES

The period following my degree will involve the completion of a Masters of Business Administration. By the time the MBA is completed, my workplace position should either be in, or leading to, a supervisory or management post. Further company-related courses will be required to enhance my knowledge of the Qantas system of management and related industrial relations.

My ultimate aim is senior management at Qantas Airways Ltd. Any industrial experience should therefore consolidate my degree studies as well as present a path to my ultimate goal.

Student: _____

Academic adviser: _____

Example 7. Clinical experience contract with prescribed competency areas

This is another example of a contract designed to be used for the clinical practice component of the course. The course is competency-based and includes a handbook with explicit assessment criteria for each of the five competency areas. The learning contract must include objectives within each area. The contract is based upon specified learning outcomes for each period of clinical placement, although students are invited to consider what they personally hope to get out the placement and write their own objectives compatible with the course requirements. Contracts are expected to build upon learning from previous placements. Ways of achieving each objective and the criteria for assessment are discussed with the clinical supervisor, and the contract signed by the student, the supervisor and the university tutor.

University of East London
Faculty of Science and Health
BSc (Hons) Physiotherapy

LEARNING CONTRACT FOR CLINICAL PRACTICE

Student: **Year:**

Dates: **to**

Type of placement and location:

Absence: (days)

Objectives	Criteria for assessment	Completed
What do I want to learn?	What are the characteristics of my performance which will show that the objective has been met?	Yes No
1. *Problem solving* (includes assessment goal setting, treatment planning, reassessment evaluation and modification)	(a) (b) (c) (d)	
2. *Treatment management* (includes application of techniques and handling skills)	(a) (b) (c) (d)	

3. *Communication*
   (with the patient)

   (a)

   (b)

   (c)

   (d)

4. *Documentation*
   (POR)

   (a)

   (b)

   (c)

   (d)

5. *Professional behaviour*
   (includes communication with PT
   colleagues and MD Team,
   appearance and CSP rules of
   professional conduct)

   (a)

   (b)

   (c)

   (d)

Learning resources
How will I learn?
(Please specify, eg, discussion with whom, observation of what, teaching sessions on ...,
reading of ...)

Method of assessment
What form will the assessment take and who will the assessor be?
(Please specify, eg, feedback from whom, observation of my practice by ..., review of my
POR by ...)

Student PT: _____ Senior PT: _____

UEL tutor _____ Date: _____

Example 8. A learning contract with set objectives

This contract specifies the required learning objectives which all students must meet for this subject. Again, the contract is designed for use during the clinical placement and is negotiated between three parties: the student, the clinical supervisor and the university tutor. Students are free to add their own objectives to those specified, based upon personal interests, and discuss with the supervisor the best way of meeting each objective listed. Regular reviews are scheduled to discuss progress and times for meeting with the supervisor are agreed at the start of the placement. The assessment column records the method of assessment only, since the criteria are common and relate to the diagnosis, treatment and evaluation of patients.

LEARNING CONTRACT: Respiratory Disorders		

Student Name: **Tutor:**

Contract Rules
Renegotiation may be implemented by student, tutor or clinical educator.
Continuous assessment of and feedback on student performance.

Learning objectives	Learning activities and resources	Evaluation
On completion of this placement, the student will be able to demonstrate:		
(a) A knowledge of the pathophysiological changes occurring in conditions affecting the respiratory system re COAD, cystic fybrosis, bronchietosis, chronic bronchitis and emphysema.		
(b) An understanding of the effects of these changes on the functional ability of patients.		
(c) A knowledge of the procedures for diagnosis and monitoring of these conditions.		
(d) A knowledge of the effects of medical care.		
(e) A knowledge of the psychological and social consequences of a slowly progressive disorder.		
(f) An ability to assess a patient appropriately.		
(g) To select, apply and adapt physiotherapeutic techniques in the treatment of patients with respiratory disorders.		
(h) To give advice and instructions for self-management.		
(i) A knowledge of the roles of other members of the health team.		
(j) An awareness of ward management and an ability to prioritize patient management in the ward.		

Signed
Student: _____ Clinical educator: _____ Tutor: _____

Example 9. Three-way learning contract for planning a work experience programme

This style of contract is more detailed than usual and is intended to be used in the planning of a work experience programme. It is a three-way contract negotiated jointly between the student, the workplace supervisor/mentor and the academic adviser. The interesting feature of this contract is the provision it makes for recording the details of the support the organization will offer in terms of resources for learning and the role of the supervisor/mentor, and the additional support which can be expected from the academic institution.

LEARNING CONTRACT

Course: _____

Student's name: _____ Phone: _____

Course coordinator: _____ Phone: _____

School/department: _____

University: _____

Supervisor/mentor: _____ Phone: _____

Organization: _____

We agree to the following:

Objectives of the
placement

Student's learning goals
and needs

Activities to be undertaken to
reach these goals

Time to complete

Assessment criteria (to be
applied by the academic
institution)

Level of support the
organization can
provide:
- resources
- time
- appropriate
  experiences

Role of workplace
supervisor/mentor

Frequency and duration
of meetings between
supervisor/mentor and student

How feedback will be
provided by the
supervisor/mentor

What additional support
and resources the
academic institution
can provide

Signed _____ Title _____ date _____

Signed _____ Title _____ date _____

Signed _____ Title _____ date _____

PART III

TAKING ACCOUNT OF LEARNERS' AND ADVISERS' NEEDS

Chapter 9

Learners' experiences of learning contracts

Students' perceptions of the use of learning contracts are many and varied. The views which have done most to inform the ideas expressed in this book are those communicated to us by students over a number of years by means of formal course evaluations, opinion surveys, informal discussions and written reflections. These students are typically mature age, studying part-time and concurrently employed within the field of adult education. They include both undergraduates and postgraduates. Some of the contracts they undertake are within specified subject areas while others are open-ended projects chosen by the individual learner. The degree of staff support provided may vary from an adviser:student ratio of 1:4 to upwards of 1:50, depending upon the course.

The overwhelming consensus among these students is that learning contracts offer significant benefits over other types of assessment and that, despite some initial difficulties in appreciating the concept, they should be retained as the major focus of learning and assessment in those courses which use the method. It is important to keep in mind that these students are responding to the particular use of learning contracts in a given context. However, their views give some indication of the kinds of feelings which students express about this approach to teaching and learning.

This extract from a student's contract describes the conflicting emotions common to many students' experiences of using learning contracts:

> My experience as a student has always been within the traditional authoritarian mode of passively receiving information in the form of a lecture, where there has always been limited or [no] choice in the topic and form of assessment... I have spent many years developing my capacities and abilities to respond to and learn within this tradition... which encourages dependence in learning.

The learning contract was a nightmare at first because it was a very different way of learning. It recognized my adulthood as an important factor in the learning process along with my experience as a woman, a worker, a member of the wider community. No longer was I a student but an adult student with a social, cultural and political history. It recognized these factors as within my individual learning process not separate or unrelated.... I am asked to make decisions as to what is relevant to my learning process. I choose its topic, its form and mode of assessment. The learning contract has shifted the responsibility of my learning from the expert lecturer to me, through choice and responsibility.

This process of transformation has been one of confusion and disorientation and a deal of self-questioning and self-doubt with many spillover effects into other areas of my life. In many ways the learning journal [which I kept] has been a map of this process.... [I]n the course of my reading I have discovered the literature often documents the process I have described as a common experience and I have taken heart at such validation (Higgs 1988)!

So why have I taken a moment to reflect on this process and given it such importance? It is extremely relevant to my facilitation practices in the work-place. The process has raised my awareness to my own needs as an adult learner, particularly in terms of environment, time and the place it has along-side my many other roles and responsibilities as an adult. More so it has shifted my place of learning towards interdependence.... To say the least, it is a very complex process.

Worthwhile learning is not without challenges. Some of these are intrinsic to any form of learning which places increasing responsibility on learners, but some challenges are unnecessary artefacts of the ways in which students have been introduced to a new process. The experiences of the students discussed in this chapter can assist in distinguishing between these and identify how learning contracts can be effectively implemented.

All data reported in this chapter, and quotations from students, are drawn from formal studies. Each list presented provides a summary in descending order of the number of responses in each category from a study of 100 students. Other details are to be found in Sampson *et al.* (1992; 1993).

Advantages

The major advantages as perceived by students are summarized as:

> Learning is of interest, value or relevance to the learner or the learner's workplace
>
> Empowering/in command of own learning/learner is responsible for learning
>
> Flexibility and scope for originality
>
> The process develops various skills
>
> No pressure of competitive marks or examinations

Motivation is higher
Freedom to choose
Able to learn at own pace, schedule around work and personal needs
Process provides focus and guidelines
Process respects individual differences
Encourages deep approaches to learning
Increased confidence and excitement in learning
The advising process

Students elaborated on these in written comments in related categories.

Contracts promote ownership and relevance
They expressed a strong sense of being in command of their learning and undertaking a project they had personally initiated and in which they had a personal investment. This in turn meant learning was seen to be more relevant to them. Comments such as the following are typical:

It's your idea, you have ownership of the experience.

The greatest advantage to me is the way the course becomes relevant to you and to your own situation.

You are meeting your own needs and in this way the course is more relevant to you.

I am able to learn in depth about a particular study area I am interested in.

For me, this is where the real learning takes place. If the topic is relevant and I need to know it, I really learn.

It is certainly the best way of completing any course. I found most of the traditional essays/exams I have done in other courses totally irrelevant to the real world. All the contracts have been interesting and have built into a useful resource, not only for now but also for the future.

The real learning starts at the end of the course when you embark on a lifetime of self-directed learning using the skills and confidence acquired here. It's not the teacher's achievement, it's your own!

Contracts encourage self-reflection
While learners are aware that contracts enable them to make connections between their course and their other interests, they may not always realize at first that the act of formulating a contract proposal requires considerable self-reflection and a questioning of motives and assumptions which may hitherto have been taken for granted. This idea was expressed by comments such as the following:

It makes me evaluate more. Why do I want to do this? What do I hope to achieve? What do others expect of me? What do I want from others?

Being responsible for developing my own study programme (with much assistance from my adviser) has forced me to review my competences, my work situation, my career expectations and aspirations. I doubt that such self-awareness would have occurred through a traditionally structured course. I feel motivated to learn rather than just fulfilling my obligations as a student.

This is a very reflective way of learning which takes into account individuals' preferred learning styles.

Great invention. The only way to learn 90 per cent of the time! It has changed my whole attitude to teaching and learning.

Through learning contracts I have discovered new skills which have changed my career path.

Empowering! Absolutely the best outcome. The process has helped me become a self-directed learner without doubt.

Disadvantages

The major student perceptions of disadvantages of the method are represented in the list below. Most comments concerned initial lack of familiarity with the approach and the time taken to negotiate a contract, particularly identifying a suitable topic. A few students referred to the sense of isolation they felt when working on a contract different to that of others. Other responses focused on problems experienced with advisers, keeping the project to a manageable size and the greater self-discipline required to implement the contract. The perceived disadvantages tended to be more varied and relate to the circumstances of each individual.

> Time required for negotiation
> Difficulty in finding a topic
> Isolation – studying alone
> Access to advisers
> Lack of formal guidelines
> Problems with adviser
> Keeping the project manageable
> Concern that it might be possible to miss topics
> Difficulty in understanding concept initially
> Need for greater self-discipline

Significantly, fewer disadvantages were mentioned than advantages. Also, each disadvantage was mentioned by fewer students. For example, nine students listed time required for negotiation and difficulty in finding a topic as disadvantages, while 64 claimed relevance and ownership as an advantage. No disadvantage was mentioned by more than nine students, while 11 advantages were mentioned by more than ten students.

Detailed comments on disadvantages ranged from common concerns, such as those above, to more personal worries which related to problems experienced by part-time students. Some students wrote of the difficulties of meeting course deadlines while studying part-time, working and raising a family, as though this was only a problem for those using learning contracts! Several respondents wrote at length on the problems they had locating high-demand books in their libraries and about the need to ensure adequate resources are available before commencing a contract. Concerns that 'other' students might try to cheat by resubmitting old contracts were also mentioned by two or three respondents, though none claimed to have actually done so personally or to have known of anyone who had. Comments tended to relate to one of the following concerns.

Initial confusion

The majority of comments concerned confusion on encountering the learning contract method for the first time. Related to this was uncertainty regarding topic selection when discussing a contract with an adviser:

> I had never heard of a learning contract before I came here so I found the whole thing very confusing and for the first few months had no idea what I was supposed to do.

> When you start the course it is a very difficult concept. It is hard to realize you actually have a choice.

> By far the hardest part was all the guesswork and feeling around. Is that what they call self-directed learning?

> I can't help but comment on the fact that in the early days some people couldn't handle learning contracts because they never knew where they were. They preferred a fixed learning agenda.

> Initial lack of direction – what to write on, what area of the topic to focus on.

> If it is a subject you know nothing about, it is hard to decide what area to focus on.

Assessment standards

Concerns about the way one is to be assessed and the assessment standards which must be met are not unique to working with learning contracts. What is different for those using contracts is that not all students are undertaking an identical assessment task. Although contracts are seldom the only means of learner assessment, and although policies regarding minimum levels of performance usually exist, assessment issues can still be worrying.

> One problem was not knowing what other students are doing or what standard is expected.

> Personally, as a learner I often write more than if it were a set assignment. This is not usually a problem for me but it can be if someone says, 'I'm just doing enough to get through'. It seems somehow unfair that a low level of effort reaps

the same reward as a high level. [This would only apply when results are ungraded.]

Some advisers approve anything and give you a standard assessment – whilst others are pedantic and negotiate the objectives several times.

The lecturers can't know everything so how can they assess a report if they are ignorant of the topic? So often they just revert to 'clarity of argument' type feedback.

More time-consuming than an essay.

Difficulties experienced and suggestions for improvement

Students were asked about difficulties they had experienced and how these had been overcome. They also made suggestions for improving the use of learning contracts.

Difficulties

The difficulties experienced are summarized as:

> Deciding on a suitable topic/defining scope/writing specific learning objectives
> Lack of familiarity with the method
> Problems at negotiation stage with adviser imposing ideas or not offering support
> Completing the contract form/wording objectives/identifying resources/setting assessment criteria
> How to make the contract interesting and challenging while condensing information
> Locating suitable resources and books when needed
> Lack of feedback on completed contract and varying standards by different advisers
> Insufficient knowledge to plan the contract in detail or specify outcomes before starting
> A feeling of being left alone
> A lack of time

Most students had experienced some problems. Half of those who had experienced difficulty identified some aspect of 'getting started' as their main area of concern. This ranged from problems of motivation and overcoming personal inertia to that of identifying a topic for a contract and then 'fitting' this idea into the contract form. In particular, setting objectives and determining assessment criteria proved most problematic, especially for students new to the contract process. This problem lessened with experience and as confidence with the method grew.

Suggestions

The strongest recommendation from students was for the learning contract process to be introduced in much greater detail, with both the theory and practice of using learning contracts discussed early, possibly within specially run workshops. It was suggested that this would be helpful not only to students but also to lecturers and advisers, among whom interpretations of the process were seen to vary.

> More detailed introduction to theory and practice of using contracts, for example during orientation workshops
> More discussion about contracts and sharing of ideas with fellow students
> Models of learning contracts available for perusal
> Greater adviser/staff involvement from the outset
> Induct session leaders and advisers more thoroughly
> Provide more reassurance, guidance and support to students
> Initially, suggest possible topics or topic areas
> Assessment criteria made more explicit
> More discussion of assessment and more detailed feedback
> More negotiation and discussion when formulating a contract
> Clearer guidelines for contracts
> More advising time

Other suggested improvements were that copies of learning contracts from previous years be made available for students to inspect and that explicit guidelines be given. At the stage of first contact with the idea, possible topics could be nominated to help students begin the process of setting their learning objectives and alleviate the dilemma of too wide a choice. Greater involvement of advisers was suggested, particularly in giving support and guidance to students and clarifying issues about assessment and feedback on contracts. Also recommended was that there be greater opportunity to discuss with and work on contracts with other students, sharing the knowledge gained. More time, it was suggested, should be spent in the negotiation phase of developing the contract, discussing the objectives, resources and assessment criteria.

Although some students raised the issue of the restricting features of different assessment criteria used in the various courses (eg, the use of word limits) there were no strong preferences regarding assessment practice nor suggestions for improvement. However the nature of the comments suggested that the rationale for different criteria was not clearly understood.

Advisers obviously play a key role in the successful implementation of the method and need to discuss their expectations, particularly in regard to assessment criteria, very clearly with learners. It is apparent that students believe that it is important to prepare both staff and students to work with contracts and to promote an educational culture which values the opportunities the method offers and the diversity of approaches it makes possible. The chapters which follow consider some strategies for introducing contracts to staff members who will be acting as advisers, and to students.

Chapter 10

Orienting advisers

In courses where learning contracts have yet to be introduced, teaching staff are likely to be interested in what the method has to offer and how it will affect the way they work with students. Some may be openly sceptical. Once learning contracts have been accepted as part of the teaching/learning process in a course or subject, staff who become advisers need to be oriented to the more specific details of negotiating and working with contracts. This chapter considers the issues which are typically raised by staff and discusses two forms of orientation: staff workshops and a course handbook suitable for both staff and students.

Issues that arise for staff

When considering introducing learning contracts there are always questions about why such a change might be warranted, exactly how learning contracts can be used, and what their introduction would mean for both students and staff. Following adoption, the issues expressed shift to the day-to-day procedures of how to work most effectively with students. Concern about workload is common, while barriers to working effectively with the method may arise from the beliefs and assumptions about learning and learners that teachers hold.

Questions typically asked include:
- When do you use learning contracts?
- What do contract proposals and completed contracts look like?
- How can you help students develop objectives and criteria for themselves?
- How do you get students to accept responsibility for their learning?
- How do you ensure that students gain the level of knowledge, under-

standing and skill required by the institution and the profession?
- How do you ensure complete content coverage in a subject?
- How can the process be used in large groups of students?
- How do you deal with a variety of levels of motivation?
- How well will they work with school-leavers who may expect lecturers and tutors to tell them what to do?
- How do you measure student performance?
- How do you determine the assessment criteria?
- How do you prove learning has taken place?
- What are staff and student roles?
- What does the staff member contract to do?

The following are some of the issues that may need to be addressed.

Implementating change

Implementation of changes to courses or subjects involves consideration of procedural matters such as obtaining institutional approval and support as well as practical matters such as gaining acceptance from those who will be affected by it. The procedural matters are specific to the institution and dependent in part on organizational preparedness for change, but practical implementation concerns are often common across contexts.

Gaining support for the introduction of the learning contract process depends on ensuring that all those involved understand:

- what the method is,
- why it is being implemented,
- how to work with the method, and
- where to find assistance when needed.

Staff also need to be able to air their thoughts about the process, their interests and their fears. Misconceptions about the practice need to be uncovered and addressed.

Influence on teaching and learning

Advisers need to consider how the method will affect the structure of their subjects and the role it will have in relation to other learning activities. For example, will lectures and seminars become learning resources for the learning contract, will the learning contract become the form of assessment accompanying a lecture course, or will the use of learning contracts replace teacher-led activities? Whether learning contracts are regarded as part of teaching and learning practices rather than assessment will also have a profound influence on perceptions.

Assessment questions

Will existing assessment procedures be suitable or will they need to be changed? Contracts are usually criterion-referenced rather than norm-referenced. This means that assessment which involves ranking or making discriminations between students is inappropriate. Will contracts be the sole basis for assessment or part of a wider sampling of the student's abilities which might include tests and assignments? How will assessments arising from learning contracts be consolidated with others forms of assessment? Learning contracts are most easily assessed as satisfactory or unsatisfactory (depending on whether or not the defined criteria have been met). However, in a course where other work is graded, it might be necessary to grade contracts to avoid the perception that they are of lesser value.

The role and responsibility of the adviser

The role of the adviser is clearly influenced by the nature of the process and encompasses different areas of responsibility: responsibility towards the learner and responsibility towards the academic standards of the institution. Role and responsibilities of the staff adviser normally include:

- initially, providing an overview of the subject and the anticipated lecture topics
- guidance – providing and stimulating ideas and suggestions
- negotiating the contract
- challenging learners' ideas
- interpreting the institution's requirements
- informing the student of non-negotiable criteria
- suggesting relevant resources
- providing reassurance, encouragement and support
- monitoring the learner's progress
- renegotiating the contract, as needed
- assessing the completed contract and giving feedback

For the individual adviser, the multiple roles of guide, encourager, negotiator, resource person, monitor and assessor may not sit comfortably, particularly when the previous roles may have been that of teacher, instructor, director and examiner. Effective advising requires staff to accept a role which emphasizes facilitating learning rather than directing it and taking seriously each student's experience and aspirations. Adjusting to this is not straightforward, and may be affected by the adviser's conceptions about learners and how learners should relate to teachers.

Even staff experienced in using learning contracts may find the dual roles of encourager and assessor present some contradictions and discomfort. This obviously involves a range of issues but it also places an emphasis on specific elements of the process such as both student and adviser being very clear about their responsibilities and the necessary procedures. In some applications of learning contracts, the roles of adviser and assessor are split between different staff members to avoid potential role conflict.

In acknowledging a different role and relationship with the learner, the adviser may still need to clarify how the process works and resolve practical issues about working with large and small groups. Of particular importance is finding ways of helping learners accept increased responsibility within the overall constraints of the course.

Advisers also need to think about how the method may alter their way of approaching teaching and their interactions with students. As students develop skills and confidence in using learning contracts, they increase their autonomy as learners and the relationship between students and teachers alters.

The role of the learner

Students are generally not used to assuming so much responsibility for their learning and they are often unfamiliar with skills such as writing learning objectives and planning learning strategies. They may also regard know-ledge of resources and assessment criteria as being the sole responsibility of the adviser. So in the early weeks of negotiating learning contracts, advisers need to appreciate that students are learning about the process, as well as the content of the subject, and may need some assistance in developing the necessary skills to proceed through the steps of developing a contract.

It is important that advisers understand how students may experience the transition to using negotiated learning contracts: the disorientation and confusion, sometimes mixed with feelings of excitement and challenge. It is the advisers who need to orient and support the students as they accept their new responsibilities as learners. To assist students in this transition there is practical help the adviser can give. This is discussed in detail in the following two chapters.

Demands on staff

The adviser's role may not be something students have experienced before and if it is not understood, confusion may result. Unlike some other meth-ods, the learning contract process requires staff to be resources, facilitators of learning rather than instructors, and work with students rather than simply telling the student what to do. Good communication skills are vital. Additional skills in negotiation, problem solving and creative thinking are also desirable in working in this area.

Being regularly available to students may also be necessary at particular stages. When and where the adviser is available, or indeed not available, needs to be clearly communicated to avoid unnecessary stress for all involved. Once students become familiar with the method they tend to make considerably fewer demands on staff time, although the relationship between student and teacher is generally less distant than in classroom-based teaching. However, teachers can also find relinquishing part of their role to students very confronting. Unless they are open to this possibility they should avoid taking on advising. For some advisers it is a process that can profoundly challenge beliefs and values about education and educational practice.

The negotiation process

The process of negotiating the contract is the most significant change for both learners and advisers. Once the learner has drafted a proposal the adviser and learner become involved in a negotiating process. They may engage in conversation with each other, either face-to-face or over the telephone. Advisers may not always be available to discuss all elements of the proposal with learners, so their communication with learners may, after initial discussions, be written. They might recommend limiting the issues to be considered or adding a specific competency or topic that would be more suitable as the focus of the learning objective. The adviser should discuss with the learner all aspects of the proposal, especially the assessment criteria. The better the relationship between the learner and the adviser the more likely it will be that the adviser can assist the learner in exploring ideas and suggesting relevant strategies and resources.

Advisers need to be aware of their position in the negotiation activity and what they stand for. Answers to questions such as, 'What is negotiable?' and, 'What is not negotiable?' need to be clear to advisers in advance so that the scope of the negotiation is clear to both parties. It is useful for advisers to be able to discuss the process of negotiation and for them to have an opportunity to practise the skills required in their negotiating role.

Negotiation factors

McCarthy (1993) suggests that when negotiating learning contracts the 'bargaining area' and the 'negotiation range' be clearly established at the outset. Other considerations for staff during the negotiation are:

- valuing the other person(s) involved
- identifying the objectives of the negotiation
- listening more than you talk
- being neutral and factual
- actively seeking mutually acceptable outcomes
- knowing the concessions that you can make
- identifying and using a colleague you can discuss the issues with.

Workshops for staff about learning contracts

Many of the questions and concerns that advisers have are often best handled in a forum with others who have used the method or who are examining the possibility of implementing it. A workshop also provides an opportunity to relate information about learning contracts to a specific course.

Rather than simply embracing the concepts and practices, most people attending preliminary workshops are wary of change and maintain a critical eye, so it is important to encourage participants to express their apprehension and listen to the views of others in a similar position. Advisers need time to consider the application of the ideas being considered to their specific courses or subjects. Similarly they may need time to voice their concerns before listening to others relating their experiences and suggest possible solutions. It is not uncommon for practical barriers to implementation to surface in these sessions. A strategy for dealing with these constraints will be necessary if advisers are to be confident in their new role. The staff workshop provides the ideal conditions to model the style of interaction that is likely to develop between student and teacher when working with learning contracts – as learning partners jointly involved in problem solving.

Although workshops need to be carefully planned with segments for delivering information, the most effective style of facilitation will be one that encourages the participants to reflect on their own contexts, contribute from their experience, express their doubts and concerns and engage in dealing with issues as they arise. Above all, workshop designs need to be flexible.

Workshop content

Although initial questions about learning contracts are well covered by reference material, beginning to negotiate with learners raises specific questions. Once basic questions have been answered about what a learning contract is and why it is to be used in the particular course, the adviser needs to become familiar with the learning contract proposal form and how it can be completed. In the spirit of negotiation the issues to be addressed should be decided with the advisers present. The more an adviser can learn about the process of negotiation as the learner might experience it, the more likely they are to understand a student's need for support and encouragement.

WORKSHOP CONTENT

The two most common forms of staff workshop are those which provide an orientation to the potential of learning contracts and those designed for staff who are already commited to being advisers. The first of these might include:

- different ways of using learning contracts
- students' experience of using learning contracts
- advantages and disadvantages of learning contracts, and
- the implications for staff and students if learning contracts are used in a particular course.

The second, considering the practicalities of advising, might explore:

- the staff and student roles in using learning contracts
- negotiating learning contracts with students
- strategies to support students using learning contracts
- staff concerns about using learning contracts.

Other issues that might form part of staff workshops when learning contracts are already in use, could be course-specific information about how learning contracts are used within the particular subject or course, how to complete the proposal forms, and what criteria are non-negotiable. Topics might also include:

- why learning contracts are used in the subject or course
- the steps in the learning contract process
- negotiating learning contracts in small and large groups
- problems that might be encountered by learners

Achieving the appropriate balance in using the learning contract method will undoubtedly be different in each learner-adviser relationship but in the staff workshop it is useful to discuss different styles of approach from directive to non-directive. When learners first begin working with the method they may be unsure about what to expect of advisers, and in finding their way they are sometimes seen to be 'lost' and in need of direction. It is tempting for an adviser to tell a learner what to learn, and what to put down as the learning objectives and strategies. To refrain from directing, and to attempt to question and explore possible areas of interest with the learner, requires considerable restraint and skill in active listening.

The procedures, the pitfalls and the implications for the adviser's role are all issues that can usefully be addressed. Throughout, it is helpful if there can be examples of learning contract proposals and completed work for advisers to examine and work with. Similarly it is preferable if advisers have opportunities to consider possible learning contract topics within their subject areas and to practise using the proposal forms with these topics in mind.

The handbook

Given that there is not enough time at the orientation stage to cover all the issues, and that many only emerge later, it is important for staff and students to have information available in a handbook format where they can access it readily. A handbook also has the potential to provide course or subject specific descriptions. The handbook might cover some general areas but essentially it could outline some of the following.

Course-specific handbook contents

- details of the area of study
- ways that students might approach their learning contracts within particular subjects
- guidelines for the subject
- suggested scope and range of the learning contract
- range of resources
- models of possible learning contract proposals
- details of where examples of completed learning contracts can be inspected
- expected word length – size of work
- assessment guidelines
- suggested time-frames or deadlines
- when and how learning contracts can be renegotiated
- issues that have been determined as non-negotiable within the particular subject or course
- strategies for ongoing support

With access to the handbook and an opportunity to discuss issues within workshops, staff are well prepared to begin working with students negotiating learning contracts. However, as they engage with the process there will undoubtedly be times when they are concerned about how they should proceed. Like students there is a need for staff to have ongoing assistance provided. This may involve having opportunities to formally discuss specific issues with others involved with the practice or the establishment of a forum at which common problems might be addressed.

Chapter 11

Orienting learners

As discussed earlier, confusion and uncertainty are common reactions when learners are first confronted with the prospect of using learning contracts. They are not sure what to expect or what is expected of them. Questions commonly asked by learners at this stage include:

- What do learning contracts look like?
- How do you work with learning contracts?
- How is the method different from other ways of working?
- What is involved?
- What is meant by 'the learner taking responsibility'?

Learning about new practices and adjusting to them takes time. In addition to being unfamiliar with the process and not knowing how to proceed, learners may be being introduced to learning contracts at the same time as they are coming to terms with new subjects and possibly a new learning environment. The questions they have about learning contracts can become intertwined with the questions they have about their programme of study generally.

Students commence their tertiary study keen to know what is expected of them and what is involved in a particular course. Some school leavers may feel sufficiently prepared, at least in part, for what lies ahead of them; others may be apprehensive about their ability to manage the volume of reading and writing they will be required to complete; while for older students this initial enthusiasm may be accompanied by concerns about re-entering education and balancing course commitments with work and family responsibilities.

Students may have heard about learning contracts from friends and colleagues but probably not used them themselves (although increasingly primary and secondary schools are encouraging more independent learning approaches). When advised that their courses do not involve examinations or traditional set assignments and that their learning is primarily assessed on work achieved through negotiated learning contracts, reactions can be mixed.

When the concepts and the processes involved in using learning contracts are first explained, most students find it reasonably straightforward. They may be excited about the challenge and the anticipated freedom to choose; however, when they begin to apply these ideas to their formal work they can experience a range of difficulties. The scope the process offers can be overwhelming, but just as worrying to the student can be concerns about filling in the contract proposal form correctly. They may feel uncomfortable, even disoriented, as they begin to work with the process. Some learners have described the experience as like being in a 'fog' and they have found themselves losing confidence in their abilities as learners.

Students are not always able to identify what is causing them to feel uncomfortable and yet their discomfort may manifest itself in quite strong emotional responses. Some students experience feelings of self-doubt and anxiety, while others can become irritated or even angry about the method and look for someone to blame, sometimes venting their hostility on their adviser. This transition and resulting disorientation needs to be acknowledged and discussed so that students can recognize that it is not a failing in themselves (or their advisers) but rather a result of the changes they are making in their approach to learning.

Addressing learners' issues

Given the significance of these changes for the learner, and recognizing that they are discovering how to approach their learning differently, it is important that the approach is systematically introduced.

In Chapter 9, students experienced in using learning contracts suggested a range of strategies which would have assisted them when learning contracts were introduced. They recommended that they be given a workshop to introduce them to the theory and practice of using learning contracts, guidelines about their use within specific subjects, and background written material about the contract method. Support from staff and fellow students was also considered important, particularly in the initial stages. To remove the air of mystery that sometimes surrounds the discussion of contracts, students requested access to model learning contract proposals and examples of completed work.

Students found it helpful to express their concerns and discuss with fellow students different ways of coping. They appreciated hearing about difficulties experienced and how they have been overcome. Discovering that they are not alone in their reactions is important in maintaining their confidence as learners.

Students' disorientation can last until they successfully complete a piece of work and receive feedback on it, so the earlier the first learning contract is attempted, assessed and returned, the easier will be the transition to this way of learning for students. It is therefore important that the first contract work be modest in extent and conducted over a relatively short time-scale. A contract of 1,000 words over one month is a better starting point than 5,000 words over a semester.

Any number of means can provide learners with the necessary information, eg a handbook similar to the one suggested for advisers in Chapter 10, participation in workshops, talking to former students, discussions with staff, or presentations in lectures or tutorials. The more varied the opportunities to learn about learning contracts, the easier the transition to this approach is likely to be. Ideally one resource will build on the next to provide learners with a reasonable understanding of the process and sufficient skills to commence working confidently.

Orientation workshops

Many of the questions that students have about using learning contracts can be addressed within an introductory workshop. The value of having a workshop as opposed to an information session is that a workshop can provide an opportunity for participants to practise the skills involved in developing learning contract proposals. It can also be used as a forum for learners to discuss their concerns, so that they can plan strategies to help themselves and each other in coping with the unfamiliar process.

Negotiation, essential to the practice of working with learning contracts, is unlikely to be familiar to students in the context of formal education and should be addressed in the workshop. The roles of learner and adviser in this process need to be clear to both parties, while students may also want to consider the issues that may inhibit them from participating comfortably in this activity, and how to overcome them. Practice sessions within a workshop can be useful in preparing students for having their ideas challenged and other ideas proffered.

Experience suggests that an orientation workshop should occupy two or three hours. Without such an introduction learners are likely to experience considerable confusion and anxiety which in turn will probably increase demands on staff time later as disoriented students seek individual assistance. Just when the workshop should be run will depend on how learning contracts are being used within the overall course. Students need time to adjust to the approach as they begin to work with it, so it is probably best to run the workshop at an early stage when students have some familiarity with the overall features of the course and are wanting to know more about how they are expected to proceed.

WORKSHOP CONTENT

The content covered will vary according to the student group and the particular course or subject. However there are some general topics that could form the basis of the workshop and these are suggested in the questions most frequently asked about learning contracts:

- What are learning contracts?
- How are they used?
- Why use them?

Other queries provide a more specific structure for the workshop. Students are concerned initially with the mechanics of working with learning contracts:

- What do learning contracts look like?
- How do I decide what to learn?
- How is the form filled in?
- How is it negotiated?
- How is it to be assessed?

Similarly, other issues to be considered may include:

- How are learning contracts different from other processes of learning and assessment?
- What benefits are derived from the process?
- What are the roles of staff and students?
- What have been experiences of students in the past?

Workshop designs

Workshop designs will obviously vary according to the experience of the group and the style of the workshop facilitator. A practical 'tell, show and try out' approach may suit some groups (see Student Workshop A) while for other learners it may be more appropriate to start by relating the learning contract method to their non-formal learning experiences and then considering the implications for a formal course (see Student Workshop B).

Student Workshop A

The first example generally takes about two hours with a group of thirty or fewer participants. Based on the questions most learners first ask about learning contracts it also provides learners with an opportunity to draft a learning contract proposal.

STUDENT WORKSHOP A

In line with the concept of learning contracts it is often useful to construct the workshop around questions that participants want answered. Beginning with the question, 'What questions do you have about learning contracts?' can provide a focus for the group. If the group is very large the following questions can be used to provide an outline for the workshop:

What is a learning contract?
Why are learning contracts used?
How are learning contracts used in this subject/course?
How is a learning contract proposal written?
Who is involved?
What is involved?

What is a learning contract?
Participants may have used learning contracts before or may have thoughts about them which could benefit other members of the group, so asking for their understanding of learning contracts is a useful first step.

A definition can be given on an overhead transparency, relating it to the participants' responses and specifying how it is used in the particular course or subject. When the term is used to refer to both the proposal and the resulting completed work it is useful to clarify this.

Why are learning contracts used?
An explanation of why learning contracts are used provides an educational rationale. Students responses about the advantages of using learning contracts (see Chapter 9) can be used to illustrate the potential benefits.

How are learning contracts used in this subject/course?
All information in the orientation session should focus on the particular form of learning contract used locally. Material about variations can be very confusing if these are not options which are available.

How is a learning contract proposal written?
Discussion of the learning contract proposal form needs to include what is expected in each column and the date agreed for completion. It is helpful to discuss each column of the proposal form in detail, giving examples of different ways of deciding on and expressing what should be included.

It can be helpful to discuss some of the following points:

- Learning objectives may need to be rewritten several times before they are achievable.
- Subject guidelines, lecturers' suggested topics, course notes, the suggested readings and discussion with fellow students may help in determining learning objectives and resources.
- The column for assessment criteria is often difficult to complete but it is important that the criteria are relevant for both adviser and learner.
- Contracts are renegotiable.

EXERCISE – DRAFTING A PROPOSAL
Copies of completed proposals are useful for learners to examine and critique before they attempt to develop a proposal.

An exercise of drafting a learning contract proposal can be done individually or in small groups. When the proposal is ready it can be swapped with other individuals or exchanged in a small group as if it were being 'submitted' for negotiation and approval. Part of the negotiation process may involve altering aspects of the proposal: suggesting other resources, seeking clarification, perhaps narrowing the objective or adding criteria to the assessment column. Students give each other feedback before examples of proposals are discussed in the larger group.

Who is involved?
Depending on the context in which learning contracts are being used, there may be staff, students and possibly workplace supervisors involved. Certainly learning contracts need not be agreements between just two people. Learners may choose to negotiate a learning contract in pairs or as a small group researching a particular topic and the staff involved may be the learners' adviser and another subject or field expert.

What is involved?
Using learning contracts affects the roles of both learners and teachers. Clarifying these roles helps all those involved.

Learners take responsibility for learning and use their initiative by:

- asking for assistance
- seeking resources
- questioning
- formulating the proposal
- fulfilling course standards
- renegotiating the contract if necessary
- timekeeping
- giving support to colleagues

Staff provide learners with:

- guidelines in course material
- clarification of what is feasible
- examples of models of what is expected of them
- ideas and challenges
- assistance in focusing
- advice about resources
- support throughout the process
- clear understanding of course standards
- constructive written feedback.

The workshop might conclude with learners considering a contract proposal about learning more about using learning contracts.

Student Workshop B

The second example describes a workshop plan which draws on learners' previous experience of learning, relating it to using contracts. It helps learners understand the elements of a learning contract proposal and the range of learning opportunities that the process offers. This approach takes about one and a half to two hours, depending on the group and how much they already know about learning contracts.

STUDENT WORKSHOP B

A general question to determine the participants' understanding of learning contracts is posed initially. Responses are recorded on a board, paper or on an overhead transparency. These responses should influence the direction and points of emphasis in what follows.

Using learners' previous experience of learning
Each participant is provided with a blank form with four columns marked Column 1, Column 2, etc (ie, a learning contract proposal form without the usual column headings).

Participants are asked to think of something that they have learned in the last 12 months that they are prepared to discuss with others. They write down in Column 1 of the form what it was that they learned. (It is easier if participants select something they intended learning.)

Examples of what they might put down should be illustrated; for example: having learned how to repair a window, feeding fish, using a computer program, buying a second-hand car or applying for entry into this course!

Next, participants are asked how they went about their learning. They write the resources and strategies used in column 2. It is likely that they will have used more than one resource and taken a number of steps. Prompts include: where they looked for information, who they talked to, or what resources they used.

Participants then fill in the remaining columns with a description of what they were able to do as a result of their learning or what they had as evidence of their learning when they had finished (column 3) and the criteria they used to determine that they had learned enough (column 4). Again, prompts are helpful.

Having documented their learning experience in this way, participants discuss what they have written down with another person or several people in a small group.

In the whole group, examples of what people had learned are invited. A variety of responses in each of the columns is recorded on the board. It is not necessary to follow one learning experience through from column 1 to column 4, but it is useful to identify and record a range of types of learning from skills-based learning to learning involving attitudinal change.

Linking learners' past experience of learning to using learning contracts
The next stage is for participants to consider how working with learning contracts may differ from the informal experiences they have just documented.

Column 1: Learning objectives. Participants discuss how they decided what they would learn and how this might differ in the context of using a learning contract. Consideration of difficulties they might experience in deciding what to learn and where they might look for guidance begins discussion about some of the issues relevant to working with learning contracts. It is appropriate at this stage to introduce how learning objectives can be written in column 1.

Column 2: Resources and strategies. Many of the resources and strategies already in column 2 may be suitable for working with learning contracts but, if there are some that are not appropriate, these need to be highlighted.

Column 3: Evidence of learning. The different forms of evidence of completion that are specific to the learning project they considered earlier, such as 'a repaired window' or 'a newly purchased second-hand car' can be noted. Participants also contribute suggestions for ways of presenting evidence of learning, drawing on other formal learning activities.

Column 4: Criteria for assessment. The criteria nominated in column 4 may also be very specific to the past learning experience, such as 'it prevented the rain coming in' or 'it suited my budget'; however other criteria acceptable in the particular context should be discussed and non-negotiable criteria listed.

Developing a learning contract proposal
Having discussed the four columns of the learning contract proposal form participants may wish to look at model proposals or attempt to complete a proposal form themselves with suggested topic areas. This can be done individually or in small groups and discussed in the larger group to clarify any misunderstandings and show the range of options available.

Chapter 12

Other strategies for assisting learners

Introductory workshops, handbooks and suitable examples are all important strategies for helping students begin to understand the process. However, students need information and guidance at different stages if they are to be effective. This chapter describes some of the issues students are confronted with and suggests approaches to assist students following initial orientation activities. These are used most effectively in combinations which suit local circumstances and time constraints.

The strategies described here are based on the assumptions that learners involved are able to meet each other face-to-face, that they are meeting with staff in class (for purposes other than negotiating contracts), that the meetings are on a regular basis, such as once a week, and that these meetings are held over eight or more weeks. However with computer conferencing, telephone links and electronic mail available, these approaches could undoubtedly be adapted to achieve similar exchanges between students who, because they are physically isolated, do not have the opportunity to meet with other learners in a group setting.

Students helping each other

As contracts are commonly individually negotiated, students may get the message that they are on their own, that learning must be done without contact with others. This impression often arises when students come from educational backgrounds in which cooperation is regarded as akin to cheating. Establishing a climate for learning where students are encouraged to support each other will help to counteract feelings of isolation and other difficulties learners experience.

Staff can do much to encourage students to support each other. Students often find their fellow students an unparalleled resource, providing support and ideas. To overcome the barriers that large groups, impersonal lectures or infrequent meetings might present, staff can recommend and initially organize strategies that bring students together beyond their required meeting times. These strategies include the use of study groups, learning partners and joint contracting. A relatively small investment of time devoted to introducing and structuring these activities can have considerable benefits later.

Study groups

Study groups are student-led meetings in which the agenda is set by the participants. They can be organized formally or informally around a subject or a whole course, with an anticipated lifetime of a semester or longer.

Formal study groups may be arranged to enable students to learn about working together within a small group as well as providing a forum for exchange about their learning and to discuss any problems they might be experiencing. Such groups allow participants time to discuss the different learning contracts they are working on and they present an opportunity for students to work together on group learning contracts or projects. Group members may also reflect on their behaviour within the group and the effect of that on the group's development.

Established by a staff member, but without staff in attendance, groups are given guidelines on how they might proceed. The purpose of the group is to establish a forum in which students are able to support each other in their studies but the responsibility for deciding exactly how the group achieves this and how it uses its meeting time is for the members of the group to determine. A requirement that the group meet regularly, for a minimum period of time, and that the group's meetings and general progress be reported to a staff coordinator, provides an element of formality.

This task focus and structure tends to overcome the concern busy students frequently have about sitting around chatting about themselves. Having a member of staff responsible for the coordination of study groups requires some accountability on the part of the groups while also providing some guidance on how to proceed and assistance in resolving conflicts that might threaten their functioning,

Informal study groups may arise from student initiatives or from a suggestion made by a lecturer or course coordinator. Just recommending that people join together in groups of three to six people to meet regularly and discuss their work, can help students take the necessary steps. Some students are not used to talking about what they are learning outside the lecture or tutorial room, particularly without a member of staff to guide the discussion. Others find it hard to allocate time to a meeting for which there are no credit points or marks. So, without initial staff impetus some would probably elect not to attend, without appreciating the value of such a process.

Learning partners

A learning partnership involves a student having regular contact with some-one else with whom they are comfortable discussing ideas that are raised in lectures or study, and with whom they can explore their own interests, exchange work for comment and generally have a friendly person upon whom they can call (Robinson *et al.*, 1985; Saberton 1985). Students can be introduced to the idea of using a learning partner at any time during a course. They are encouraged, though not required, to choose another member of the class to act as their partner. The formalization of this arrange-ment is particularly important for part-time students or members of non-dominant social groups who do not have the same opportunities for peer interaction as others. Students are encouraged to meet for coffee or make their own arrangements for how they might maintain contact and work together. This could involve computer or telephone links or meeting before or after class.

In organizing learning partners, students may be asked to exchange infor-mation about themselves so that people with similar interests can be matched or so they can select their own partners. Criteria for matching may be arbi-trary or quite specific such as living in the same area or being interested in the same topics in the subject being studied. The linking of students in this way with some guidance as to how they might proceed provides a loose struc-ture that gives them encouragement to talk about what they are learning, what they are understanding and failing to understand, and any difficulties they are encountering in using learning contracts.

Joint contracting

Students can negotiate to work with a partner or group of fellow students on a learning contract. Although it is possible that students may elect to work together because of a mutual interest in a topic, it is more likely that before they venture into a joint contract they have already established a relation-ship, possibly from working as learning partners or as members of a study group. Certainly how they intend working together needs to be established before they begin. The benefits of working with others in this way generally extend beyond learning about the topic alone, to learning about working cooperatively and coping with differences.

Staff working with students

Staff obviously play a major role in initiating strategies that assist learners to develop their ideas and maintain motivation. They provide guidance by suggesting possible areas of study and suitable resources and it is with a member of staff that the student negotiates and renegotiates the learning contract proposal. Again it is a member of staff who provides feedback on the completed work and finally accounts for the student's progression through the course.

In some courses it may be possible for staff to work with students in small groups or even one-to-one relationships as tutors or academic advisers. In such situations students can explore their ideas about what they might study and how they might approach it, and receive direct feedback from the staff member.

Records of student work

If learners proceed through a course involving a number of contracts, they are likely to work with advisers who may not know what they have studied previously. To assist in understanding a student's progress and development, there needs to be a record of the topics studied and the competences gained. This record may be organized and kept centrally by the department or institution or may be kept more informally by students. It is normally a document compiled by each learner and shown to advisers at the time of contract negotiation. The form in which it is presented is sometimes referred to as a Record of Learning Achievements or a Learning Log.

Some courses require the learners to maintain a very detailed account of the work they complete, not simply listing the contracts they have undertaken but providing a description of each contract, the extent of the contract, its relationship to different subjects and what has been learned from it. If these details are combined with copies of completed contract proposal forms, the work itself and the adviser's feedback, learners have a much fuller documentation of their learning than they can get from other types of courses.

When students maintain this record they often find the process of summarizing the evidence a worthwhile activity in itself. They are able to see what they have achieved and how far they have progressed. Students also find it useful as a means of portraying what they have learned to prospective employers.

Using class time to support learning contracts

Lectures may be the one period of time in which all students undertaking contracts are gathered together. There are various strategies which can be used within a lecture to help students benefit from the experience of their fellow students and extend their ideas about areas of study.

Clarifying ideas about topics for contracts

One activity, based on an idea from Knowles (1975), involves students working in groups of three for approximately 15 minutes to discuss possible learning contract topics. This can occur no matter what the size of the total class might be. It might typically form part of the class or lecture session in the second or third week of meetings.

Each student has five minutes to talk about his or her ideas. One student begins by giving a brief description of what his or her topic might be, then a second student asks a series of questions about what has been proposed. Through this process of questions and answers the original ideas can become more focused and other ideas considered. The third student observes the discussion and later reports on what he or she has seen and heard, adding yet another perspective to the discussion. Each student takes it in turn to present his or her proposals, and act as proposer, questioner and observer.

Before these discussions the students may not have formed any definite ideas about what they want to study, but in the five-minute sessions that can be the focus of the discussion. Simply by being asked questions, the learner begins to think about his or her interests. Sometimes by discussing topics he or she does not want to pursue, the student begins to clarify which topics are clearly not of interest and which might present a challenge.

Students are often surprised by what emerges from these discussions and find that their ideas become clearer as they discuss them and listen to the ideas of their colleagues. If, after the groups of three have discussed their thoughts, suggestions are brought to the larger group, even more ideas can be generated.

At the end of the three-way discussions it can be useful for students to frame their thoughts by writing a draft learning contract proposal. This is not necessarily the final learning contract proposal but it helps in the development of the contract to be submitted later. Even if it subsequently changes, preparation of this draft presses the learner to start thinking about a contract in a purposeful way.

The following week, students spend ten minutes exchanging draft proposals, asking for clarification and giving each other feedback. This again triggers ideas and may result in more alterations to the draft. The reviewed draft proposal is then submitted to the lecturer for his or her comment or approval and the negotiation process begins.

Later in the semester, once the proposals have been negotiated and accepted, time can be allocated in a lecture for students to discuss in pairs or threes how they are progressing with their contracted work. If a student feels comfortable about colleagues seeing their work they can bring drafts to class to be read, listened to and viewed by other students who could ask questions or seek clarification about it. While these discussions help students develop their ideas, they also help maintain interest in what they are working on.

Trying out ideas before final submission

Often within a field of study it is necessary for learners to develop skills in presenting ideas and knowledge in specific ways. This may restrict the way in which the evidence of learning is presented for a particular contract. For example, it may be considered necessary for all students in a subject to learn to present data within a report structure, or perhaps it is relevant that they know how to write a case study or a critical incident.

Although the format might be determined, there is still an opportunity for choice within such a contract because the student remains responsible for the selection of the content of the particular case study or critical incident, and for deciding what is to be analysed and critiqued within it.

This approach presents two learning challenges for the student: learning about the content of the topic and learning about the specific format in which it is to be presented. To assist students, the proposed material can be brought to a lecture and discussed by students in twos and threes, then different examples can be selected for discussion in the large group before being sub-mitted for negotiation and approval. For each of the different examples, ways of approaching the material can be suggested so that everyone devel-ops an understanding of what is expected of them.

A draft of final work can be brought to class for further exchange and dis-cussion or it can be submitted directly to the lecturer/adviser for comment, before the work is completed. Using this method, students are supported throughout their learning and the dual challenge for the student of learning about the content and the format is addressed.

Opportunities for exchange

Students have suggested that there should be opportunities to learn about the work that others in their class group are doing in their learning contracts (Anderson *et al.*, 1992). This may be achieved by using the approaches already discussed. However, it may also be useful to establish a centrally-situated resource room where completed learning contracts can be located and made available for others to look at. This may not always be appropriate as some work may contain confidential or personal material.

Another possibility is to hold a seminar towards the end of the semester in which students present a brief overview of the work they have completed. In this way they can discuss both the content of their work and the process they used while also maintaining control of the material they make public. The seminar might be part of the lecture programme or an additional meeting designed specifically for this exchange.

Chapter 13

Organizational implementation

The introduction of any learner-centred approach will challenge a department or institution with a predominantly teacher- or subject-centred culture. Learning contracts are sufficiently flexible in their application that they can provide simultaneously an explicit structure and organizing framework for study which takes into account academic and professional standards, and a means of responding to student diversity and a variety of learning needs in a way which gives students significant influence over their study. The approach they represent can reassure staff who are concerned about handing too much control over to learners as well as providing sufficient scope for those who wish to give students greater responsibility for their learning. It is possible to build an alliance of both groups around the idea of learning contracts. Depending on which group exerts the most influence, contracts can be structured in a looser or more rigid manner. This is reflected in the examples discussed in Chapter 8.

However, there are a number of more practical concerns which need to be addressed by educational managers. The main resource issues concerning how to make the learning contract approach work within an organizational context are discussed below.

Time constraints

To work well the learning contract method demands an investment of time at the negotiation stage and a further commitment by the adviser to provide ongoing advice and support as required. Time will also be needed to assess each individual project and this may take longer than applying standard criteria to a set assignment. However, there are likely to be time savings at other stages in the course as learners are working on their own learning plans.

Students new to contracts will require considerably more assistance than those experienced in their use, but in all cases some discussion needs to occur before the actual learning project begins. Depending upon their familiarity with the subject matter, learners will require differing levels of advice and support as the project proceeds. Managing the process through regular consultations with learners and arranging group meetings or seminars are important parts of the adviser's role. Advisers and their departments need to make time allowances for this.

Learners also will experience time pressures. The ability to manage one's time effectively is probably more important with a learning contract than with more prescribed assignments. There is a common tendency to expand the original topic to include new ideas and themes encountered during the research. If learners have a personal commitment to the topic they may find it difficult, even undesirable, to limit their thinking and reading solely to the contracted objectives. The final product may also be more extensive than originally envisaged. Occasionally a learner may abandon their first idea and seek approval to begin a new contract, creating further time demands. Advisers therefore need to ensure the learner is not attempting something too ambitious or is not proposing an activity which is unlikely to be fully realized in the time available. Of course the common tendency to leave assignments until the last minute also afflicts users of learning contracts, except in this case the nature of the task may mean the limited time remaining is insufficient to do justice to the negotiated agreement. Learners should be advised to commence their reading and other preparatory activities as early as possible to avoid having to renegotiate the contract or request an extension of time. This is important for advisers, as they need to manage their own time. Students should also be encouraged to develop a plan for pacing their activities over the timescale available, keeping in mind that they will not be able to envisage in advance all the demands of their plan.

Allocating staff time

The level of one-to-one consultation available to learners will depend upon various factors, such as the number of students enrolled in a course, the adviser's workload, the individual needs of each learner and the resources available. Time-saving methods are usually available or are soon devised by those working with learning contracts. For instance, communication by phone, fax or e-mail can serve as a convenient substitute for personal interviews in many situations, especially when arranging mutually convenient appointments is difficult. Variations on the basic approach, as described later, can also be tried.

A learning contract, in its purest sense, can be used as a substitute for lectures or other sections of the curriculum. Learners identify their own relevant learning needs and plan a programme to address these needs, which may or may not include attendance at formal classes. In this case a lecturer may negotiate effectively with 25–30 students. The use of individual projects, in which learners negotiate a contract to explore subject areas independently, can also contribute to course credit yet require minimal staff involvement. In such cases one adviser can typically supervise up to 50 students each semester as part of a normal teaching load.

Having one adviser take full responsibility for all contracts undertaken in a particular stage or module has a number of advantages, not the least of which is consistency of assessment. This also frees other staff for regular teaching commitments or to act as specialist advisers for particular subjects. Another option is to appoint a contract coordinator, who manages the learning contracts across the course, ensuring each student completes a balanced set of contracts, and recording dates of submission, results, etc on behalf of the department.

Cost factors

One of the most commonly asked questions at staff workshops, typically by heads of department or course leaders, is 'How can we adopt what appears to be a highly resource-intensive form of teaching?' The simple answer is that many departments with similar funding levels to their own have managed to do it successfully: all those who have adopted this approach have found some way to make it work within their own system. Stephenson (1988), for example, reported that the use of learning contracts for the whole of a degree programme was undertaken at a less favourable staff:student ratio than the average within his institution. In education at the University of Technology, Sydney, learning contracts are used as the main learning and assessment vehicle in a school funded at around the average level for schools of its type. However, this raises questions of the specific demands that learning contracts place on staff time and other institutional resources and how this time can be budgeted.

While the overall demand of learning contracts can readily be accommodated, this does not mean to say that the introduction of contracts in one aspect of an otherwise unchanged course will not create pressure on staff resources. The main reason for such difficulties is that the work-load demands on staff do not follow the same pattern as conventional teaching. Less time is require during some parts of the year and more at others.

Typical pattern of time spent by staff in a subject exclusively using learning contracts compared to conventional teaching

Less time than a lecture course:	*More* time than a lecture course:
Before the start of the course in overall preparation (lectures, handouts and assignments do not have to be prepared in advance, although briefing and orientation activities need to be designed and guidelines updated)	On one-to-one or group negotiation with learners at the initial stages (the first three to five weeks)
On contact with learners during the term, as they are working on their own learning plans. There is some troubleshooting and renegotiation required, but this typically involves less than would be required for normal teaching	Possibly on assessment, in providing specific feedback in terms of the contract. (This may or may not take more time depending on which assessment practices are being compared)

While there are variations depending on the types of contract used and the familiarity of students with the process, there are typically two peaks in staff workload: at the time of orientation and negotiation of contracts and at the time of assessment. For the rest of the time, the load is significantly less than in regular teaching activities; there is some follow-up and renegotiation, but this would typically take less time than would be spent in lectures and tutorials.

Workloads can be allocated so that as far as possible staff take roughly equal shares of contract supervision. In education at the University of Technology, Sydney, for example, for working with educationally disadvantaged learners using contracts and meeting university study for the first time, staff are allocated the equivalent of 20 minutes per week per student as part of an overall load of 10–14 hours per week. This reduces as students become more adept in using the contract approach, and in later stages of undergraduate courses. At the postgraduate level, staff are allocated the same load they would have had if they were teaching the same number of students in a lecture/tutorial format. Class sizes are normally kept below 30 and, in common with other schools adopting a more learner-centred approach (see, for example, Ryan and Little, 1991), there is not the same pattern of significant reductions in class size from first to final year that is common in lecture-based departments.

Laycock and Stephenson (1993) propose an alternative to this practice. They suggest:

> A switch from hourly-based, weekly-accounted staff management to case-load annual timetabling [which] would (a) recognise the peaks and troughs in tutoring student-managed learning, leaving staff with alternating busy and fallow periods consistent with the distinctive sequence of varying student needs which student learning implies and (b) suggest a totally different perspective from which to judge the issue of resource-intensiveness (p.163).

As far as other resources are concerned, there are no significant differences in cost. Access to a good library is required in contract learning as much as in any form of university study and the fact that different students are focusing on different aspects of a given topic can mean that the demand on texts is spread more widely than would be the case if all students were undertaking the same assignment.

PART IV

EXTENDING THE RANGE OF LEARNING CONTRACTS

Chapter 14

Variations in use

The types of contracts discussed so far may not always be suitable for certain courses or learning situations. This chapter presents some alternative ways in which learning contracts may be used. The essential feature of all the options presented here is that the emphasis remains on meeting identified learning needs and allowing each learner as much autonomy as possible in a given context. What follows are some examples of both minor and major variations to the basic model. A minor variation retains the key features of the contract method but introduces some type of restriction, shortcut or local practice for the convenience of either the students or the advisers, or both. A more substantial variation introduces an additional element to the standard approach, such as negotiations with a number of learners at the same time.

The main varieties considered here relate to contracts developed within a particular academic subject area, contracts negotiated with a group of learners, and contracts intended to plan or supplement a complete course.

Learning contracts within a subject or module

Since most learning contracts are undertaken within a designated subject or course module, teachers may wish to ensure all learners have completed similar work and understand the main content knowledge associated with their subject. For this reason they may place restrictions on what is negotiable in terms of either the topic or the expected outcomes. For example, a contract may have many learning objectives pre-specified, leaving the student to determine exactly how they will be achieved (see example in Chapter 8). At the other extreme, the learner may draft an entire contract prior to consulting an adviser. Of course, it may be argued that in cases involving either imposed limitations or total learner independence, some basic features of negotiated learning are absent. However, this need not be the case. All learning contracts involve a balance between the learner's freedom to choose and the imposed requirements of the course: in the examples below it is just that the balance has shifted slightly one way or the other.

Pre-drafted contracts

Staff resources may not allow for every learner to negotiate every part of a learning contract from scratch through one-to-one discussion. The most common approach, and the one favoured by Malcolm Knowles, is for learners to draft a complete learning contract and then submit this for approval prior to commencing their activities. This saves time for both the learner and the adviser, but does require some familiarity with the course requirements as well as confidence in drafting learning contracts. Even so, not all advisers will accept a pre-drafted contract since they feel it undermines the two-way dialogue the method is supposed to promote. It remains, however, a popular option with larger classes or when wishing to acknowledge the right of an experienced learner to make the initial decisions. A pre-drafted contract does not change the need for registration, the adviser simply responds to it.

Restricted contracts

If the contract is to form a major part of the assessment for a particular subject or module, restrictions may need to be placed upon either the content, the expected end product, or both. This is to ensure comparable subject coverage and fair assessment between learners. At other times particular activities, for example, working in a group or consulting set texts, may be prescribed for all participants. Some advisers may also insist on viewing draft work before the final product is submitted for assessment. These restrictions, limitations or other requirements will need to be explained fully and contracts negotiated within the parameters set.

In the early stages of a course, one or two model contracts, specifying objectives and outcomes, are sometimes developed with a group of new learners to ensure that foundation skills and knowledge are covered by everyone. If the learning objectives are prescribed in advance, the learner is then free to negotiate learning strategies and assessment criteria in the usual manner. This can be a useful option with skill-based subjects or those which include a period of practical experience. In such cases the representative of the educational institution will set the learning objectives and the remainder of the contract can be negotiated with the field supervisor.

Model or sample contracts are also useful in orientating new learners to the method or in courses in which students typically submit very similar contracts. This is frequently the case where the course has a high factual, technical or skill-based component and all students aspire to an equivalent level of mastery. In these cases sample contracts can be supplied by the lecturer/adviser, with students being encouraged to choose from among these as a starting point. At other times the model serves to provide guidelines for types of topics, outcomes and quality standards expected in learning contracts prepared for a particular course. Negotiations can then proceed based on individual preferences in regard to learning strategies, resources, depth of treatment, credit sought and assessment criteria. Having sample contracts available can also do much to alleviate initial confusion.

Graded contracts

Many courses use graded assessments and may select students for progression into the later stages based upon these grades. This practice does not preclude the use of a learning contract for assessment purposes. A learning contract can be marked and graded in the same way as any other assignment or assessment task. However, there are some specific issues which need to be considered.

First, assigning a grade to a piece of negotiated work might seem to be at odds with the idea of independent, learner-centred learning. If the adviser also acts as assessor there may be, for some, a degree of role conflict (the support role versus the evaluative role) especially if a number of the adviser's students are competing against each other for marks.

Second, it introduces an element of competition between students. Students may be inclined to select topics they feel will score the highest grades rather than explore areas of genuine interest. The learning contract may be oriented to please the assessor rather than the learner. Students can spend considerable time trying to discern the preferences, interests and biases of the assessor. While a certain amount of second-guessing probably occurs in any case, there seems little point in encouraging the practice through the system itself.

Third, it can be difficult to assign a percentage score or grade to independent work. What may be a major achievement for one learner may represent very little work on the part of another. The basic criterion for a good contract is how well the learning experience has met the needs of the person concerned, not how well it compares with what others are doing.

Finally, if the focus of the contract becomes the final grade there is no reason for students not to contract in areas in which they may already have considerable skill or knowledge. Perhaps the student who sets out to learn something new will be disadvantaged. This is not an appropriate use of learning contracts.

Nonetheless, these problems are not insurmountable. Assessment mechanisms can be devised to ensure the essential features of contract learning are retained while still allowing the contracts to be graded. For example, if grades must be allocated, one solution is to contract for the grade *before* the work is completed. One possible approach, first suggested by Hiemstra and Sisco (1990), is offered below.

GRADED LEARNING CONTRACTS

Six basic elements contribute to negotiating a graded learning contract which could be used within most courses. These can be summarized as follows:

1. The student discusses with the academic adviser what is required to achieve a preferred grade (typically an A or B, or distinction or credit) for the subject concerned.
2. The adviser makes his or her expectations clear from the outset. Quality requirements are spelt out. This may even include points of style in the written presentation or how many hours of work a particular grade might represent.
3. A list of objectives is prepared and the student agrees that *all* the objectives must be achieved for the grade to be awarded. If not, a lower grade may be allocated.
4. The objectives may be renegotiated for a higher or lower grade at any stage during the life of the contract, or the original objectives may be modified if mutually agreed.
5. The adviser retains the right to assign a grade which reflects the quality of the work submitted.
6. The student may be given the option to rework and resubmit items not up to the agreed standard.

If learning contracts are to be graded it is necessary to have a detailed assessment policy across the course or subject. Assessment criteria for each of the grade divisions for each type of assessed work need to be explicit and the qualities of work which would merit a particular grade made clear to students. One suggestion is to maintain a small library of previously submitted contracts which are good examples of acceptable work for each available grade. Students could then study these model contracts before determining their own assessment preferences.

Independent contracts

Learners may sometimes be allowed to undertake a learning contract of their own choice as a full unit within a particular course. In this case there is considerable freedom to select topic areas and assessment products relevant to the interests of the person concerned, although some general requirements are normally imposed to ensure a comparable workload for all individuals.

The role of the adviser and times for consultation will also need to be established. It is not possible to state categorically how much time a learner should spend negotiating and discussing an independent contract with the adviser. Confident learners may only seek initial agreement to their contract and not consult again until they have nearly completed the project. Others will require ongoing support or will prefer to obtain more regular feedback as they proceed. Similarly, the adviser may insist on continuous discussion and monitoring or may encourage learners to take a more self-directed approach.

Progressive or serial contracts

One method particularly useful with new learners is to build up a series of contracts, beginning with small, set contracts, until the point is reached where the learners can negotiate a more substantial independent contract. A sample contract can be used as a model during the early stages or the adviser may work through each section of a contract with the class as a whole to illustrate the process. In this way all learners will begin with the same contract and gradually identify areas they wish to explore in more detail for themselves. A variation on this approach is to have learners progress from limited contracts to fully independent projects within the same topic area, each piece of work building upon and extending the one before.

At other times, learners may contract to undertake a series of assignments or projects in order to develop an important topic more fully or because of a desire to specialize in a particular field. A series of linked contracts is then drafted as the course progresses. Alternatively, a more general contract is prepared initially and subsequent work related to this. This option is mainly used in specialist postgraduate programmes. By the end of the course the learner will have built a substantial set of related contracts which should prove a valuable resource in their future work.

Group learning contracts

In courses where a large number of learners are undertaking a similar assignment, it may be more convenient to negotiate a common contract with the learners as a group. Indeed, unless reasonable staff resources are available, this may be a necessity.

The idea of group contracts merges with the idea of the negotiated curriculum, on which there is an extensive literature (for example, Boud and Prosser, 1980; Harber and Meighan, 1986; Millar et al., 1986). While contracting is often a feature of courses which are jointly planned by learners and teachers, the tradition from which these have emerged is quite different from the emphasis on individualization found in the tradition which has produced learning contracts. Other writers have emphasized joint planning and taking of responsibility for conducting courses, such as Torbert's (1976) 'community of inquiry', Heron's (1974) 'peer learning community', and Boydell's (1976) 'experimenting community', though these have mainly been used outside the context of formally assessed courses.

Large group contracts

Contracting with a large group normally starts with a specification of the expectations and assumptions which the faculty or department holds for the group. For example, it may be assumed that all group members have the necessary academic prerequisites, that all have completed certain subjects or come from similar work backgrounds. It may be expected that certain things will occur by a certain date or that all learners will benefit in a given way from undertaking the contract. These assumptions and expectations apply to all members of the group and hence need to be made explicit to all before details of the contract are discussed. In other words, the common learning needs of the group and the reason for undertaking the contract need to be made clear if each person is to be convinced of the value of the exercise.

Similarly, the learning objectives and the required outcomes will be provided in a general form to the group, with individuals matching these with their own personal goals, intended strategies and learning resources. Some minor modifications to objectives and outcomes may be allowed depending upon individual circumstances. Learners should also be ·encouraged to expand upon and extend the common objectives. However, despite any additions or modifications, each learner is still expected to demonstrate competence in the core areas as a minimum course requirement.

During the briefing sessions these requirements are dealt with and a 'typical' contract developed with the group. Learners then have the option of working from this model or drafting their own version for approval by the staff adviser. If a very large number of learners are involved, or if the department insists on common outcomes or common procedures, restrictions may be imposed upon how free any individual is to vary the agreed model. The process may be represented as follows.

Steps in developing contracts with a group

1. Initial student briefing in group.
2. Discussion of learning objectives by group.
3. Suggested learning strategies and resources through group discussion.
4. Agreement of outcomes and assessment criteria by group.
5. Discussion of model contracts in group.
6. Development of individual contracts.

7. Final agreement of contracts with advisers.
8. Implementation of contracts.
9. Assessment of individual contracts by advisers.
10. Final debriefing in group.

Although each learner will have received individual feedback and assessment from an adviser, it is still important to debrief the group at the end of the project. Apart from providing a sense of closure, this meeting is also an opportunity for staff to gain feedback on the success of the learning contract method and for group members to exchange ideas and concerns and to identify further learning needs which may have become apparent.

Small group learning contracts

With a smaller group, such as a tutorial class, a project group or a study group of about six to eight people, it is possible for the group members to initiate the contract themselves. Contracts between three to five students can sometimes be used when others are contracting on a one-to-one basis.

For instance, if the group is required to undertake a particular project they may first seek agreement among themselves about their desired goals and intended outcomes and then proceed to discuss possible ways to achieve these outcomes. The role of the staff adviser is to advise the group as necessary while the contract is being developed, provide formal approval of the contract and assess the final product. In other words, the contracting process occurs in the usual sequence but the individuals within the group must first reach agreement before seeking final approval from the staff adviser.

This type of contract is useful in courses which include a large practical, design or task component. Using material from classes and elsewhere, small groups of learners work together on a project which they then present for assessment as credit in that course. Examples would include groups who have worked together on a corporate business plan, an advertising campaign or a computer software program. In some cases the results are presented to the larger class and their fellow learners provide feedback and peer assessment.

The group contract can overcome a sense of isolation which some students find uncomfortable when working entirely on their own. It also fosters a spirit of teamwork and cooperation which in a restricted use of learning contracts can tend to be neglected. When using group negotiated learning in a context of otherwise individual assessment it may be necessary for specific students to take responsibiltiy for particular identified aspects of the work and for these to be individually assessed. However, combinations of self, peer and group assessment may be used for group products (see, for example, Brew, 1995).

Complete-course learning contracts

While learning contracts are most frequently encountered within a particular subject or as a means of planning an individualized project, it is possible to use them to negotiate an entire course. There is usually an assumption in such cases that the learner would have appropriate conceptual frameworks and an understanding of criteria for assessment at different levels and relevant institutional policies and regulations in order for the contract to be valid and meaningful. Hence they are used most commonly with postgraduate students to plan higher degree programmes. Recently, however, some universities have used learning contracts as the basis for planning complete undergraduate degrees in different courses in collaboration with major industry employers.

Course planning contracts

Malcolm Knowles, in his book *Using Learning Contracts* (1986) provides examples of undergraduate contracts constructed by students, either individually or in pairs, to plan their own programme within the guidelines provided by their instructors. In some cases the instructor's guidelines and objectives are also open to negotiation. Knowles also describes a number of degree programmes at both undergraduate and postgraduate level in which students determine their course of study through negotiation with an adviser and by matching subject areas with their own particular learning needs.

Courses designed for mature age students may recognize previous learning and experience to enable each student to tailor a course of study appropriate to their situation. This usually involves credit for undertaking existing subjects but some institutions also allow students to design a unique programme through negotiated learning contracts. The School of Independent Studies at the Polytechnic of East London (until its reorganization in 1991) offered courses of independent study at various levels, from diploma to Master's degree, based upon the accepted learning plans students developed during their first year (Stephenson, 1988). The remainder of the programme was then devised in consultation with an academic adviser.

Contracting for a degree or diploma

This type of exercise involves a detailed consideration of the following factors:

- a personal profile which includes previous education, work experience and training, present skills and knowledge relevant to the course, demonstrated competences, career goals and personal referees;
- a full description of the proposed course of study. This could include

learning objectives, areas of study, methods of study, reading lists, time-tables, etc;
- resource requirements (staff, equipment, facilities);
- a justification for the proposed study programme;
- the proposed assessment scheme (methods and criteria).

At present a number of universities in Britain, including the universities of Leeds, North London and Portsmouth (Brew, 1993) use learning contracts as the basis for tailoring courses to meet the needs of students and local industry and which lead eventually to a full degree. Saddington (1992) describes several other university courses in the USA and Britain based upon independent projects or individualized programmes using learning contracts as the means for determining both content and outcomes. These range from a short contract outlining the course aims and options to complex documents specifying complete academic programmes.

Summary

Despite the variations and adaptations which are possible, essentially what distinguishes a negotiated learning contract from other types of projects or assessment methods is the focus on the particular needs of the learner. How far the idea of a learning contract can be stretched is a matter for debate but the ideal model centred around full and honest discussion between learner and adviser will, for many teachers, remain just that – an ideal (although one worth pursuing). In this case alternative approaches can still be explored, particularly when existing practices are not serving the learner well. The learning contract method is flexible enough to accommodate most learners and can be adapted to fit most courses.

The main variations currently in use are summarized as follows.

VARIATIONS IN THE USE OF LEARNING CONTRACTS

Type	*Appropriate use*
Pre-drafted contracts	Minimize negotiation time when students are experienced with contracts and know the area they wish to work in.
Restricted contracts	When particular objectives and assessment criteria are non-negotiable.
Graded contracts	When it is institutional policy to use grades for assessment purposes or the context does not allow for competency-based assessment.
Independent contracts	As a substitute for studying a particular course unit in a conventional manner.
Progressive contracts	As part of a sequence to build towards a fully learner-driven, independent contract, *or* as part of a series of contracts which, taken together, meet the course requirements.
Group contracts	When cooperative learning is the goal and also to avoid a continuous programme of individualized learning which could isolate students from each other.
Course contracts	Students design an entire course.

Chapter 15

Applications in work-based learning

One of the most effective ways to utilize learning contracts in higher education is to base them upon the field of practice in which the learner is involved. If the learner is currently employed, this may be done quite easily by deliberately selecting workplace assignments as a learning tool and planning how experiences gained there can meet learning needs relevant to the formal course. Another common approach is to draft a learning contract prior to undertaking a period of field experience or work placement during a full-time course. This has the dual benefit of providing a definite learning focus for the student during his or her placement (something which may otherwise not occur) and of involving the workplace supervisors more directly (and accountably) in the learning component of the placement.

A key advantage of using learning contracts in connection with work experience is that it is possible to identify a full range of resources available for learning within a specific setting at a specific time. In fact many advisers would suggest that the contract need not be developed until such resources have been located, perhaps a few days or weeks into the placement. This makes it possible to plan realistic learning objectives which take full advantage of the opportunities the placement presents, as opposed to relying on incidental learning which occurs more or less randomly. The planning should also involve the learner's work supervisor in addition to the educational adviser. This supervisor, as a party to the learning contract, has more incentive to ensure the learning objectives are met and that the student is not assigned inappropriate tasks. Involving the supervisor in assessment, by means of a final report to the student's adviser, is a logical adjunct to such an approach and most supervisors are prepared to undertake this task.

Learning contracts can also be used beneficially for personal and career development or as part of a formal staff development scheme, often in conjunction with a course at a university or further education college.

The three-way learning contract

A three-way contract is suitable for formalizing and structuring the practical components of a professional course such as field placements, clinical experience, industry visits and teaching practicums. Indeed most of the recent literature concerning learning contracts reports their use with students undertaking such external assignments, particularly in fields such as nursing, engineering, information science and business management (Stephenson and Laycock, 1993) or pastoral care (Walker and Boud, 1994).

A work-based learning contract typically includes an employer or workplace supervisor as the third party but in fact anyone with an interest in the learner's progress could be involved, such as a more experienced work colleague prepared to act as mentor. In this situation the contract is developed in the usual way but with three people – the learner, the adviser and the workplace supervisor – discussing the objectives, strategies and intended outcomes. While all three should be present at the initial discussions, further drafts of the contract may be developed by the learner in consultation with either of the others (normally the workplace representative). Naturally the agreement of the remaining person should be sought if any major changes are proposed. The prime requirement is for all parties to be fully committed to the learning process.

This type of contract involves learners in determining:

- *what* they want to learn while working in the organization (this will be limited by what the university/college and the employer see as the purpose of the placement);
- *where* and *when* they will be able to learn (eg, frequency and duration of meetings with mentor, opportunities for skill development);
- *how* they want to learn (eg, practical experience, set tasks, reading, on-the-job training, member of project team, etc).

Some of these options will of course be restricted by the resources and support available to the student outside the college or university environment, including time available for consultations with the supervisor or mentor.

The quality of work experience programmes is largely dependent on the willingness of the workplace supervisor to recognize that the student is there primarily as a learner and not merely as a source of labour. A learning contract negotiated at the beginning of a placement is one way of reinforcing this point and of gaining some commitment to a planned programme of relevant practical experiences. Providing a sympathetic co-worker or mentor to assist the student's formal learning is therefore a useful part of the process. This person can be included as the major learning resource when developing the contract.

In addition to identifying the specific roles and tasks the learner will be undertaking during work experience, issues of personal and professional development can also be addressed. Such issues might include personal relations, communications, initiatives, contributions to a team, workplace ethics, understanding an organization's culture, professional responsibility and accountability. In this way the time spent at work can become a genuine learning experience and be more fully integrated into the formal academic part of the course. It can also give a greater understanding of the personal attributes which form the basis of professional competence.

For full benefits to accrue from the experience, a proper briefing and debriefing should occur with the student, supervisor and academic adviser. The learning contract can be a valuable means of focusing these discussions and for ensuring all relevant concerns have been identified. As well as specifying the intended learning outcomes, the contract ensures the student is able to demonstrate that learning has in fact occurred. This is often done through displaying a certain level of competence in the workplace or through a formal written report after the work experience. Each party therefore has a role to play which can be made explicit in the written learning contract.

Of course the learning should not be regarded as simply a one-way process. In a successful placement the employing organization should gain new ideas, techniques, etc from the student, and the university or college will benefit from direct contact with the workplace. These learning outcomes should be mutually acknowledged during the debriefing at the end of the placement.

Learning contracts with external sponsorship or assessment

It is also possible to negotiate contracts between an educational institution, an individual learner and a sponsor. In this case, the learner is working in an external location but is not acting in a work-related capacity. For example, students undertaking project work and historical research for a degree in history found placements with local libraries, museums, historical societies and private companies which enabled them to complete individual projects based upon materials available in these organizations (Nicholls, 1992). In each case a learning contract involving the three parties was drawn up to specify the scope of the projects and the manner in which they would be assessed. Apart from the student's report upon completion, various activities were undertaken during the project under the guidance of the sponsor. The result was usually a product useful for the sponsor (eg, a computer database, catalogues of archival material, historical information packs, library displays, promotional videos, etc) and the sponsor played an integral role in the final assessment. The student was able to negotiate at the contract stage the distribution and weighting of marks for the various components of the project.

Another way in which a third party may become involved is as an expert assessor. In this case the third person may or may not be involved in the original contract discussions but will have agreed to review the final product and provide evaluative feedback. This option is particularly useful when the academic adviser is not an expert in the field of study or when an outside opinion might be valuable. Another staff member with particular expertise, someone working in a particular industry or even a potential employer may be approached to comment on the completed contract and thus provide both a different perspective and a degree of specialist knowledge. In some cases a reporting proforma is provided for this person to complete which can then become the basis for the final assessment. Practicums for trainee teachers frequently use this method.

Sandwich courses and cooperative education

Sandwich courses (or cooperative education as the idea is called in North America) are based upon the principle that integrating periods of work experience into a degree course provides students with relevant industrial, business or professional experience to ensure both practical competence and an understanding of their chosen field. However, planning and assessing these periods of work experience, which may last up to a year, have never been easy. Consequently the benefits of the experience tend to be dependent on factors such as the willingness of the employer to provide suitable learning opportunities, over which neither the student nor the institution has much control.

A learning contract is one way to address this problem. A three-way contract would aim to define the student's roles and expectations together with the learning opportunities the organization could provide. Specific objectives and means of assessing them can then be tailored to the opportunities and resources available. The academic tutor can approve the final contract and regularly review progress with the student and the workplace supervisor. Gammie and Hornby (1994), in research involving 120 placements, report this type of approach has been received very favourably by all parties, including employers, and can be of considerable assistance in planning and structuring long periods of employment between stages of a degree. Regular review meetings and detailed assessment criteria are important features, while maintaining a personal learning journal, log book or diary can also be a useful aid to learning and evaluation.

Gammie and Hornby emphasize that the final assessment should identify all the skills and competences acquired during the placement and relate these to previously agreed guidelines. The guidelines serve to help plan specific learning objectives in areas such as:

- technical knowledge
- staff relations
- planning and organizing skills
- communication skills
- personal and professional qualities.

On the basis of the negotiated objectives, an action plan, including review periods, can then be developed to cover the whole of the placement, regardless of its length.

Staff development contracts

These types of contracts, sometimes called personal development plans, may be used as part of a formal staff appraisal system but can also be linked to an external course. Employees who are learners in the workplace are in a quite different position to students undertaking a period of work experience. The rapidly changing nature of most jobs means learning and relearning is now essential for career survival. A learning contract, particularly when part of a structured career development scheme, helps to provide direction and purpose to workplace learning opportunities.

While most organizations which use learning contracts at present tend to restrict their application to managerial staff or executive trainees, there is no reason why the technique could not be utilized at any level within an organization.

Professional development contracts

As with academic learning contracts, the approach to planning a professional development contract is essentially one of identifying individual learning needs, although the learning programme may be very long-term. It begins with analysing the employee's current level of competence and relating this to the skills, knowledge or experience needed for his or her future work. For career development purposes, the discussions between the staff member and the manager or mentor should also cover career aspirations and learning opportunities. Unlike a training course in which the learner may be a recipient of other people's knowledge, the contract method involves all participants directly and personally.

According to Boak and Stephenson (1987a; b) a developmental programme based upon a learning contract would normally involve:

- active support and encouragement from management
- a programme centred on the learning needs of the individual
- the identification of current skills and abilities
- the determination of future career goals (long- and short-term)
- relevant activities, projects and assignments to assist personal development
- flexibility in terms of time and location for activities
- ongoing support from a personal mentor
- a record of achievements to use as evidence of learning
- agreement to the plan by all parties involved.

There are a number of advantages to using learning contracts with staff as part of their career development. For example, Boak and Stephenson suggest that if individuals take the initiative in choosing areas they consider to be relevant to their own career goals, their motivation to learn is likely to be enhanced and they are more likely to be committed to action. Furthermore, the staff member and the employer can be involved together in formulating an individual learning programme based upon clear objectives and defined performance measures. The workplace can be seen as a site of learning and new skills developed as an ordinary part of work. This can be important in breaking down the false distinction between learning as something that happens 'on a course' and learning that occurs in the workplace.

Frequently, a planned professional development programme involves attendance at formal classes, usually at a university, college or professional institution. In this case it is desirable for a teacher from the institution to also be involved in formulating the contract. Knowles *et al.* (1986) and Stephenson and Laycock (1993) provide several examples of three-way contracts aimed at managerial and professional development and involving either a college or a professional association together with the learner and a workplace mentor.

Learning plans

One approach currently in use in some larger organizations involves a supervisor and a staff member in a career planning interview which may lead to the development of an individualized learning plan. This is very similar to a contract, but perhaps less formal or focused more on short-term goals. The process involves a number of stages, as illustrated in the model below which has been used in the Australian Taxation Office.

DEVELOPING A LEARNING PLAN

Step 1   Review your section's business plan with your manager and identify the parts you will contribute to.

Step 2   Draft a plan with your manager that outlines the specific tasks you will be performing over the next six months. Agree to the relative priorities of the tasks.

Step 3   Try to predict any likely changes in your job over the next two years. Identify any other jobs or positions you might be applying for.

Step 4   Review the competences relevant to your job. Given the business plan and your own career plans, identify any new skills, knowledge or experience you may require.

Step 5   Determine which areas of learning are the most important. Identify ways in which you might learn the things you need to know.

Step 6   Consider how your manager can help your learning. Identify other people and resources available to assist. Decide how you will know when you have achieved your goals.

A learning plan is completed to record the decisions made during the interview. Although the section headings may differ slightly, this document closely resembles a learning contract. For instance, steps 5 and 6 are borrowed directly from the learning contract method, while the first four steps are simply a procedure for determining learning needs. Of course this type of planning means that evidence of achievement of the agreed goals is an important item to be reviewed at subsequent interviews. In this way the next learning plan can be developed based upon achievements to date.

Whatever form the contract or learning plan takes, the focus is very much upon negotiating an individual career plan which involves a series of developmental activities and which is monitored and assessed by a workplace mentor. This person is not necessarily the learner's immediate supervisor (and it could be argued that it is better if it is not the supervisor) but will be an experienced person with whom the learner can consult, seek advice and plan a realistic learning strategy. Personal rapport is obviously an important consideration when selecting a mentor and for this reason alone the learner should be allowed considerable choice in the matter.

Project contracts

Short training courses and workshops conducted by colleges, universities and commercial providers cannot usually offer the chance for participants to practise the skills or learning they have acquired in an authentic setting or over an extended period of time. For this reason an assignment or project may be undertaken once the participant returns to the workplace. This project, which may extend over several weeks or even months, is later reported to and assessed by the workshop provider. Accreditation of the participant for completing both the 'practical' and 'theoretical' components of the training can then follow.

Training providers who make use of a post-course project often negotiate the activity by means of a learning contract. Here the learning objectives are related to the original course objectives but have a more specific and practical focus. The learning resources can be located in the participant's own environment, supported by whatever materials or personal contact the course provider can arrange. Most importantly, the final product needs to be clearly defined in terms of both content and format. For example, is it a requirement to provide the actual work or documents which have been developed or will a written or oral report suffice? What standard is expected in terms of quality and quantity? What degree of detail is required? What presentation requirements exist?

Having negotiated and agreed to the outcomes, a date for completion and submission must be determined. This should be flexible enough to allow for other contingencies yet should also be sufficiently soon to enable the project to be a real follow-on from the course itself. The contract is then signed and a copy retained by both parties. A third copy may be sent to the participant's supervisor if that person's cooperation is necessary for the outcomes to be achieved. As with other learning contracts, the various components of a post-course learning contract may be renegotiated if circumstances change.

A variation on the formal project contract is the agreed action plan. Here course participants negotiate with the trainer or with other participants an action plan for the next three or six month period following the course. Objectives are set and outcomes identified, together with an indication of how these outcomes will be achieved. At the end of the period both parties contact each other to discuss progress towards the agreed goals. The fact that the plan has been developed as a 'contract' with another person is a considerable incentive to actually achieve the stated outcomes.

Chapter 16

Limits to learning contracts

Learning contracts must be judged not only by what they deliver in the best circumstances, but what is possible in the typical context. This can limit their use in practice. Just as multiple-choice tests can in principle be used to test a wide range of achievements, but in practice too often succeed in rewarding rote learning, so learning contracts can help students work with others and encourage substantial initiatives in promoting learner autonomy, but often lapse into an accountability procedure for the recording of student projects. Learning contracts can do much more, but to achieve this, attention must be given both to the guidelines and strategies represented in this book and to the context in which teachers and learners operate.

Those who have experienced learning contracts seldom want to return to more traditional forms of learning and assessment. The method is popular with both students and advisers and, for many, helps them to develop an independence in learning which will serve them well throughout life. Learning contracts have been described as 'the chief mechanism used as an enhancement of self-direction in learning' (Brookfield, 1986) and as the approach 'most congruent with the assumptions we make about adults as learners' (Knowles *et al.*, 1986). However, this guide would not be complete without consideration of where contracts are appropriately used.

If subject matter is totally new to learners and does not build on their prior experience, or if the course is highly technical or skills-based and requires frequent systematic feedback to the learner, then learning contracts may be less appropriate than other methods. Piper and Wilson (1993) also point out that negotiation depends on a mutual framework of understanding between students and advisers:

> it is axiomatic that relationships of contract are dependent on the existence of shared knowledge, values and assumptions. In relation to learning contracts this means that students cannot enter a meaningful contract without a reasonable awareness of both relevant procedures and regulations and also of the academic and conceptual framework within which they are intending to work. (p.41)

There are other issues, however, which are not so obvious and yet can be of concern to those working with contracts for the first time. Some of these concern learners, such as their levels of motivation, their cultural backgrounds, their feelings of isolation and their ability to control their learning. Others have to do with the notion of negotiated learning in general. There are no simple solutions to these problems and much will depend upon the awareness and responsiveness of course coordinators and advisers to ensure that learning contracts are used in ways which are sensitive to the very diverse needs of learners.

Motivation and preparedness

While learning contracts provide an excellent opportunity to interest and motivate learners, they cannot guarantee that all will respond favourably. Learners more comfortable with traditional educational methods, those who prefer set assignments, and those who distrust innovation generally, may be hesitant to embrace contracts unless their orientation to them has been persuasive and has addressed their concerns. Others may be too immature to take full advantage of the freedom offered them. In many first-year undergraduate courses the majority of learners are young and have had little experience of different learning approaches. Some will be unwilling participants, having failed to gain admission to their preferred course or only enrolling because of parental or other pressure. Such learners may prefer a more disciplined and directive approach than that offered by learning contracts. It can never be assumed that all learners will wish to use learning contracts, even following thorough orientation.

Understandably, an enforced contract is hardly the preferred remedy of advisers committed to the idea of individual choice. There is another reason for not forcing a reluctant learner to negotiate a contract: not all learners will have the necessary prerequisite skills to do so. The temptation to simply follow the adviser's suggestions, regardless of personal preferences, will be strong. Entering into a negotiation with a staff member perceived (rightly or wrongly) as articulate, knowledgeable and powerful is a daunting prospect for many learners. Some degree of self-confidence and verbal communication skills are basic requirements of the learning contract method. Other students may face language or cultural barriers which make the idea of negotiating learning threatening. Under such circumstances it may be wise to offer alternatives.

For all these reasons it is sometimes recommended that learning contracts not be negotiated until the adviser is aware of the cultural, educational and, perhaps, personal backgrounds of the learners with whom they will be working. In many courses contracts are not used until later years of a course, by which time the challenges which students pose should have been identified.

Cultural and social barriers

The learning contract method has its antecedents in a particular cultural milieu. In multicultural societies (which include most English-speaking nations in the world today) staff may be faced with a type of resistance to the idea of negotiated learning which has its basis in language and culture. The individualistic nature of most learning contracts, and the communication skills required to develop and negotiate the contract proposal, may present real difficulties for some learners. For instance, there may be a belief that the adviser is the expert and the student is simply there to acquire knowledge. Others may feel that to question the adviser is disrespectful, or that admitting to gaps in one's knowledge will result in loss of face. Some, used to the security and anonymity of working and learning in a group, may feel anxious once the spotlight is on them as an individual. Still others, used to highly formalized classes, may even suspect the adviser is deliberately using contracts as a way of avoiding teaching. Such learners could have cause to resent the method from the outset.

Similarly, a lack of confidence in proposing or discussing learning plans may act as a significant barrier for overseas students grappling with a new language in a foreign setting. A new and confusing method of learning may compound problems already experienced.

Some critics feel the method has a strong socio-economic bias, seeing in learning contracts a reflection of the values and aspirations of educated, middle-class, white society. The method, they claim, promotes an excessive individualism which could lead to an unwillingness to accommodate others, work cooperatively or even confront social or political issues. It emerged from a North American context which celebrated the individual over everything and took for granted the notion of contractual obligations. The practice was founded on the ideal of free individuals engaging with each other to produce mutually satisfying outcomes. It can be seen as a form of what is becoming known as the 'new contractualism'.

Control and power

There is an inherent tension between the idea of learning unique to a person and external recognition for completion of an accredited course. In a sense the role of the adviser in learning contracts is to resolve this conflict as far as possible. This raises the question of who controls the process – the learner, the adviser or the awarding institution.

There can be a temptation on the part of advisers to decide the form of the learning contract, even to the extent of dictating whole sections of it. While at times this may be partially acceptable (see the examples in Chapters 8 and

14), there is always a danger that advisers take over too much. Advisers negotiating yet another contract on a familiar topic with a learner lacking ideas may simply offer a solution to a problem which the learner has not recognized. To do so negates the principal benefit of the learning contract approach, that of significant learner control and commitment. The learner must be satisfied that the contract reflects a real learning need and that the area of study selected has relevance to his or her own personal or professional development. If this is not the case, they are merely undertaking another prescribed assessment task. Some learning contracts draw so little on students' perceptions of their needs that they are, in effect, disguised assignments imposed by the adviser. While learners may be quite happy to work this way, particularly if it saves them time or worry, they are not being encouraged to accept responsibility for their own learning nor to develop skills needed for lifelong learning (Candy, 1991; Candy *et al.*, 1994). Courses in which advisers work in this way should cease the pretence of using learning contracts and instead offer clear directions for the assignments required.

Notwithstanding their intrinsic differences of role, learners and advisers can easily misunderstand the other's perspective. Learners, eager to pursue some topic of special interest to them, may consider the adviser's suggestions or requirements as restrictive and not in keeping with the spirit of taking responsibility. They may feel the adviser is trying to impose his or her own ideas without regard for their preferences. For their part, advisers may fail to consider the background of the learner and view a contract proposal with misgivings if it fails to meet their expectations for the course.

Despite the ways in which it has been portrayed in the literature, not least because Knowles' original guide was called *Self-Directed Learning* (1975), the contract method is not primarily about self-directed learning. A learning contract is a *negotiated* agreement which seeks to balance formal course requirements with individual learning needs. The extent to which it does this will depend on the negotiating skills of both parties, including, at times, a willingness to compromise and express expectations clearly and honestly. Negotiating a learning contract can be difficult simply because it calls for a level of communication different from that normally encountered in staff-student interactions. People used to traditional ways of operating are challenged by new notions of control and cooperation. Relationships of power are intrinsic to the nature of the student/teacher relationship, whatever the context, and learning contracts are not immune from these influences. The inhibiting effects on students in such relationships must be recognized.

Most reservations about learning contracts relate to acceptance of the notion of self-directed learning generally. The use of contracts assumes a willingness on the part of learners to take a large measure of responsibility for their learning and while many are happy to do so, others are more reluctant, even resistant. To assume all adults are naturally self-directed in their learning (or even should be), and that this should form the starting point for all considerations of teaching and learning, is a dubious proposition. One of the main criticisms levelled at the Knowlesian approach to learning contracts concerns this generalization (Brookfield, 1984; 1985). The imposition of this particular model may undermine the confidence of learners who have hitherto been content with their existing orientation to teaching and learning.

The 'learning objectives' and 'assessment criteria' of a learning contract can look a lot like the behavioural objectives and performance criteria of the mechanistic, systematized approaches to group training inherited from government and the military. Moreover, the 'humanistic' facade of learner-centred, negotiated learning may in fact disguise attempts to mould people in approved organizational or institutional ways (Newman, 1994). Who determines what a learner 'needs' to learn in any case? Who decides the value of the learning or the quality of the final product?

The individualistic nature of the most common approach to learning contracts raises further questions about the pedagogical and cultural assumptions which underpin the method. The freedom the method purports to offer to learners can be viewed as disempowering rather than empowering if it raises uncertainties as to how the learner is 'supposed' to behave or what exactly 'they' (the assessors) are looking for (see, for example, Foley, 1992: 145). With set assignments this doubt arises less frequently, since controls and limits are usually defined. In any case, just how 'free' a person can be in an institutional setting, or in society generally, is a fundamental question which raises more issues than advisers may wish to confront. It is not our aim in a practical guide of this nature to explore such issues further, yet they should be acknowledged as legitimate and sometimes problematic concerns.

Unfortunately, for many, the realities of higher education do not conform to the ideal context in which learning contracts can flourish. Students are often not able to negotiate freely with staff. Status and power relations influence these transactions, whether the parties are aware of them or not. In the end, students need to conform to the expectations of the institution in which they are enrolled if they are to gain the recognition which it can give. It cannot be assumed that students are necessarily well placed to determine what is in their own educational interests. They have obligations to others, they are involved in complex relationships with other individuals, with their peer groups and with families. They have ambitions which influence expectations, and financial commitments to meet if they are to remain as students. They may have neither the time nor the energy to joyfully pursue their preferred options and may elect instead to take an easier, if less rewarding, path.

In defence of the use of learning contracts, it is possible to point to many examples of highly successful contract work in courses which are not notably individualistic (nursing and health science, for example, has been one field to make extensive use of contracts). Moreover, learning contracts are frequently introduced for the very reason that the learners are *not* middle-class, competitive nor even particularly well educated. Learning contracts' suitability for use with diverse groups of learners and their ability to provide unique learning and assessment opportunities mean that those normally disadvantaged by existing educational systems can be catered for. Group work, peer support mechanisms, personal learning plans and staff commitment to the idea of tailoring the courses to suit the learners, mean many 'second chance' students (eg, mature age, special entry, disadvantaged) can be given opportunities through the use of negotiated learning contracts which would otherwise be denied to them. The authors of this guide use contracts in just such a context and would find it difficult to cater for the huge diversity of undergraduate students that they meet in any other way.

Towards learner autonomy and interdependence

By introducing the idea of negotiated learning gradually and systematically, initial fears can be dispelled and learners usually become keen to take advantage of the scope offered to construct their own learning agenda. Even in traditionally more prescriptive disciplines such as engineering and science, the chance to work on projects of personal interest is a great source of motivation for most students, and negotiated learning contracts can be used alongside other assessment tasks to good effect.

Many of the concerns teachers and learners may have about learning contracts can be addressed through the ways in which learning contracts are incorporated into a course, by making implicit assumptions explicit, and avoiding the rhetoric about self-direction and learner control which has been used to oversell the idea. Some of the principled objections are simply groundless in practice. What must be judged is what people do with the idea and how it is experienced by learners. This should be the focus for further development of this practice.

If education is about developing people as learners, then it is concerned with enabling students to meet their learning needs throughout life, whether in their work or elsewhere, and in providing a basic set of intellectual and personal skills which are essential for survival in a changing world. Content or technique alone is not sufficient. Developing learner autonomy is a central purpose of all our educational endeavours (for a fuller discussion of this idea, see Boud, 1988).

Autonomy does not mean that students work alone, in isolation from others. It does not mean there is no role for the traditional lecture, seminar or tutorial class, nor that teachers abdicate their responsibility for teaching and instead become merely counsellors, supervisors or facilitators. It does not involve removing structured teaching or discarding all that has gone before. It means a reappraisal of what teachers do in terms of content, processes and assessment. It requires learners to take more responsibility for learning and to see the process of learning as central to their education.

The use of learning contracts *alone* will not develop in learners the ability to cope with the changes they will inevitably face in their careers, nor equip them to meet all their learning needs in the future. It is however a robust strategy which can provide an impetus in the right direction.

References

Anderson, G, Boud, D and Sampson, J (1992) 'Encouraging effective learning contracts', *Research and Development in Higher Education*, 15, 578–85.

Anderson, G, Boud, D and Sampson, J (1994) 'Expectations of quality in the use of learning contracts', *Capability: The International Journal of Capability in Higher Education*, 1, 1, 22–31.

Boak, G and Stephenson, M (1987a) 'Management learning contracts: from theory to practice: Part 1 – Theory', *Journal of European Industrial Training*, 11, 4, 4–6.

Boak, G and Stephenson, M (1987b) 'Management learning contracts: from theory to practice: Part 2 – Practice', *Journal of European Industrial Training*, 11, 6, 17–20.

Boud, D (1988) 'Moving towards autonomy', in Boud, D (ed.) *Developing Student Autonomy in Learning*, 2nd edn, London: Kogan Page, 17–39.

Boud, D (1992) 'The use of self-assessment schedules in negotiating learning', *Studies in Higher Education*, 17, 2, 185–200.

Boud, D (1995) *Enhancing Learning through Self-assessment*, London: Kogan Page.

Boud, D and Prosser, M T (1980) 'Sharing responsibility: staff-student cooperation in learning', *British Journal of Educational Technology*, 11, 1, 24–35.

Boydell, T (1976) *Experiential Learning*, Manchester Monographs No. 5, Manchester: Department of Adult and Higher Education, University of Manchester.

Brew, A (1993) 'The Partnership Degree programme: idea to reality', *Research and Development in Higher Education*, 14, 264–71.

Brew, A (1995) 'Self-assessment in different domains', in Boud, D, *Enhancing Learning through Self-assessment*, London: Kogan Page, 129–54.

Brookfield, S (1984) 'Self-directed adult learning: a critical paradigm', *Adult Education Quarterly*, 35, 2, 59–71.

Brookfield, S (1985) *Self-Directed Learning: From Theory to Practice*, San Francisco, CA: Jossey-Bass.

Brookfield, S (1986) *Understanding and Facilitating Adult Learning*, San Francisco, CA: Jossey-Bass.

Caffarella, R S and O'Donnell, J M (1991), 'Judging the quality of work-related, self-directed learning', *Adult Education Quarterly*, 42, 1, 17–29.

Candy, P (1991) *Self-Direction for Life-Long Learning: A Comprehensive Guide to Theory and Practice*, San Francisco, CA: Jossey-Bass.

Candy, P, Crebert, G and O'Leary, J (1994) *Developing Lifelong Learners through Undergraduate Education*, National Board of Employment Education and Training, Commissioned Report No 28, Canberra: Australian Government Publishing Service.

Cross, V (1992) *Using Learning Contracts in Clinical Education*, Birmingham: Queen Elizabeth School of Physiotherapy.

Foley, G (1992) 'Self-directed learning', in Gonczi, A. (ed.) *Developing a Competent Workforce*, Leabrook, South Australia: National Centre for Vocational Education Research.

Gammie, E and Hornby, W (1994) 'Learning contracts and sandwich education', *Capability: The International Journal of Capability in Higher Education*, 1, 2, 46–58.

Hansen, A (1991) 'Establishing a teaching/learning contract', in Christensen, C R, Garvin, D A and Sweet, A (eds), *Education for Judgement: The Artistry of Discussion Leadership*, Cambridge, Mass.: Harvard Business School Press, 123–35.

Harber, C and Meighan, R (1986) 'A case study of democratic learning in teacher education', *Educational Review*, 38, 3, 273–82.

Heron, J (1974) *The Concept of a Peer Learning Community*, Guildford: Human Potential Research Project, University of Surrey.

Hiemstra, R and Sisco, B (1990) *Individualising Instruction*, San Francisco, CA: Jossey-Bass.

Higgs, J (1988) 'Planning learning experiences to promote autonomous learning', in Boud, D (ed) *Developing Student Autonomy in Learning*, 2nd edn, London: Kogan Page, 40–58.

Knowles, M S (1975) *Self-Directed Learning: A Guide for Learners and Teachers*, New York: Association Press.

Knowles, M S (1990) *The Adult Learner: A Neglected Species*, 4th edn, Houston, Tex: Gulf Publishing.

Knowles, M S and Associates (1986) *Using Learning Contracts*, San Francisco, CA: Jossey-Bass.

Laycock, M and Stephenson, J (1993) 'The place and potential use of learning contracts in higher education', in Stephenson, J and Laycock, M (eds) *Using Learning Contracts in Higher Education*, London: Kogan Page, 159–74.

McCarthy, M (1993) 'Factors affecting negotiation', in Stephenson, J and Laycock, M (eds) *Using Learning Contracts in Higher Education*, London: Kogan Page, 32–6.

Marton, F, Hounsell, D and Entwistle, N (eds) (1984), *The Experience of Learning*, Edinburgh: Scottish Academic Press.

Millar, C, Morphet, T and Saddington, T (1986) 'Curriculum negotiation in professional adult education', *Journal of Curriculum Studies*, 18, 4, 429–43.

Newman, M (1994) *Defining the Enemy*, Sydney: Stewart Victor Publishing.

Nicholls, D (1992) 'Learning contracts in history projects by independent study', in Baume, D and Brown, S (eds) *Learning Contracts: Volume Two. Some Practical Examples*, SCED Paper 72, Birmingham: Standing Conference on Educational Development, 7–18.

Piper, J and Wilson, E (1993) 'Negotiating complete programmes of study', in Stephenson, J and Laycock, M (eds) *Using Learning Contracts in Higher Education*, London: Kogan Page, 40–5.

Robinson, J, Saberton, S and Griffin, V (1985) *Learning Partnerships: Interdependent Learning in Adult Education*, Toronto: Department of Adult Education, Ontario Institute for Studies in Education.

Russell, A L, Creedy, D and Davis, J (1994) 'The use of contract learning in PBL', in Chen, S E, Cowdroy, R M, Kingsland, A J and Ostwald, M J (eds) *Reflections on Problem Based Learning*, Campbelltown, NSW, Australia: Problem Based Learning Network.

Ryan, G and Little, P (1991) 'Innovation in a nursing curriculum: a process of change', in Boud, D and Feletti, G (eds) *The Challenge of Problem-Based Learning*, London: Kogan Page, 111–21.

Saberton, S (1985) 'Learning partnerships', *HERDSA News*, 7, 1, 3–5.

Saddington, T (1992) 'The use of learning contracts in higher education', in Brown, S and Baume, D (eds) *Learning Contracts: Volume One. A Theoretical Perspective. SCED Paper 71*, Birmingham: Standing Conference on Educational Development, 31–40.

Sampson, J, Anderson, G and Boud, D (1992) 'Participating in educational decisions: students' experience of the use of learning contracts', in *Adult Education for a Democratic Culture*, papers from the 32nd National Conference of the Australian Association of Adult and Community Education, Canberra: AAACE, 1–10.

Sampson, J, Anderson, G and Boud, D (1993) 'Engaging with diversity: using learning contracts to link the needs of students, work and academic programs', *Research and Development in Higher Education*, 16, 311–16.

Smith, R M (1983) *Learning How to Learn: Applied Theory for Adults*, Buckingham: Open University Press.

Stephenson, J (1988) 'The experience of independent study at North East London Polytechnic', in Boud, D (ed) *Developing Student Autonomy in Learning*, 2nd edn, London: Kogan Page, 17–39.

Stephenson, J and Laycock, M (1993) 'Learning contracts: scope and rationale', in Stephenson, J and Laycock, M (eds) *Using Learning Contracts in Higher Education*, London: Kogan Page, 17–25.

Stephenson, J and Weil, S (1992) *Quality in Learning: A Capability Approach in Higher Education*, London: Kogan Page.

Torbert, W R (1976) *Creating a Community of Inquiry: Conflict, Collaboration, Transformation*, London: John Wiley.

Tough, A (1979) *The Adults' Learning Projects: A Fresh Approach to Theory and Practice in Adult Education*, Toronto: Ontario Institute for Studies in Education.

Walker, D and Boud, D (1994) 'Learning from the pastoral placement', *Ministry, Society and Theology*, 8, 1, 7–21.

Further reading

There are many reports of the successful use of learning contracts in educational and professional journals and several books dealing with learner-centred approaches devote space to learning contracts. The publications listed below offer the reader a choice of perspectives and extend the ideas presented in this book. While the lists are not exhaustive, they indicate the scope of the work which has been done in this field.

Learning contracts as an approach to learning

The use of learning contracts in negotiated and self-directed learning is the subject of the books and research papers which follow. The materials range from general, introductory works to more detailed considerations of what the method entails and how it may be implemented in educational contexts. Most authors consider both the benefits and the possible limitations of using learning contracts. Key sources are marked with an asterisk.

Barlow, R M (1974) 'An experiment with learning contracts', *Journal of Higher Education*, 45, 441–50.

Baume, C and Baume, D (1992) 'Guidance to students on writing a learning contract and having it validated', in Baume, D and Brown, S (eds) *Learning Contracts: Volume Two. Some Practical Examples, SCED Paper 72*, Birmingham: Standing Conference on Educational Development, 33–42.

Baume, D and Brown, S (eds) (1992) *Learning Contracts: Volume Two. Some Practical Examples, SCED Paper 72*, Birmingham: Standing Conference on Educational Development.

Berte, N R (ed.) (1975) *Individualizing Education through Contract Learning*, Alabama, GA: University of Alabama Press.*

Berte, N R (ed.) (1975) 'Individualizing education by learning contracts', *New Directions for Higher Education, No. 10*, San Francisco, CA: Jossey-Bass.

Bilorusky, J and Butler, H (1975) 'Beyond contract curricula to improvisational learning', in Berte, N R (ed.) *Individualizing Education through Contract Learning*, Alabama, GA: University of Alabama Press, 144–72.

Brown, S (1992) 'A workshop on learning contracts: method as message', in Baume, D and Brown, S (eds) *Learning Contracts: Volume Two. Some Practical Examples, SCED Paper 72*, Birmingham: Standing Conference on Educational Development, 61–6.

Brown, S and Baume, D (eds) (1992) *Learning Contracts: Volume One. A Theoretical Perspective, SCED Paper 71*, Birmingham: Standing Conference on Educational Development.

Buzzell, N and Roman, O (1981) 'Preparing for contract learning', in Boud, D (ed.) *Developing Student Autonomy in Learning*, London: Kogan Page, 135–44.

Caffarella, R S (1983) 'Fostering self-directed learning in post-secondary education: the use of learning contracts', *Lifelong Learning*, 7, 3, 7–10, 25–6.

Caffarella, R S and Caffarella, E P (1986) 'Self-directedness and learning contracts in adult education', *Adult Education Quarterly*, 36, 4, 226–34.

Eldred, M (1984) 'An external undergraduate degree program', in Knowles, M S and Associates, *Andragogy in Action*, San Francisco, CA: Jossey-Bass, 131–40.

Fox, R D and West, R F (1983) 'Developing student competence in lifelong learning: the contract learning approach', *Medical Education*, 17, 247–53.

Gold, J (1992) 'Learning to learn through learning contracts', in Baume, D and Brown, S (eds), *Learning Contracts: Volume Two, Some Practical Examples, SCED Paper 72*,Birmingham: Standing Conference on Educational Development., 19–32.

Goldman, G (1978) 'Contract teaching of academic skills', *Journal of Consulting Psychology*, 25, 320–24.

Gosling, D (1993) 'Informal learning contracts for skills development in seminars', in Stephenson, J and Laycock, M (eds) *Using Learning Contracts in Higher Education*, London: Kogan Page, 57–66.

Hiemstra, R and Sisco, B (1990) *Individualising Instruction*, San Francisco, CA: Jossey-Bass.

Jones, T (1993) 'Negotiation as a learning tool for tutors and students', in Stephenson, J and Laycock, M (eds) *Using Learning Contracts in Higher Education*, London: Kogan Page, 37–9.

Kasworm, C E (1984) 'An examination of self-directed contract learning as an instructional strategy', *Innovative Higher Education*, 8, 1, 45–54.

Knowles, M S (1975) *Self-directed Learning: A Guide for Learners And Teachers*, Chicago, IL: Follett.*

Knowles, M S and Associates (1986) *Using Learning Contracts*, San Francisco, CA: Jossey-Bass.*

Lane, D (1988) 'Using learning contracts: pitfalls and benefits for adult learners', *Training and Development in Australia*, 15, 1, 7–9.

Laycock, M (1992) 'Negotiated learning contracts: participatory democracy in higher education', in Baume, D and Brown, S (eds) *Learning Contracts: Volume Two, Some Practical Examples, SCED Paper 72*, Birmingham: Standing Conference on Educational Development, 43–6.

Laycock, M and Stephenson, J (1993) 'The place and potential use of learning contracts in higher education', in Stephenson, J and Laycock, M (eds) *Using Learning Contracts in Higher Education*, London: Kogan Page, 159–74.

McCarthy, M (1993) 'Factors affecting negotiation', in Stephenson, J and Laycock, M (eds) *Using Learning Contracts in Higher Education*, London: Kogan Page, 32–6.

O'Donnell, J M and Caffarella, R S (1990) 'Learning contracts', in Galbraith, M W (ed.) *Adult Learning Methods: A Guide for Effective Instruction*, Malabar, Fla: Krieger Publishing, 133–60.

O'Reilly, D (1993) 'Negotiating in an institutional context', in Stephenson, J and Laycock, M (eds) *Using Learning Contracts in Higher Education*, London: Kogan Page, 46–54.

Paul, V and Shaw, M (1992) 'A practical guide to introducing contract learning', in Brown, S and Baume, D (eds) *Learning Contracts: Volume One, A Theoretical Perspective, SCED Paper 71*, Birmingham: Standing Conference on Educational Development, 7–30.

Piper, J and Wilson, E (1993) 'Negotiating complete programmes of study', in Stephenson, J and Laycock, M (eds) *Using Learning Contracts in Higher Education*, London: Kogan Page, 40–5.

Race, P (1992) 'Not a learning contract', in Brown, S and Baume, D (eds) *Learning Contracts: Volume One, A Theoretical Perspective, SCED Paper 71*, Birmingham: Standing Conference on Educational Development, 41–56.

Russell, A L, Creedy, D and Davis, J 'The use of contract learning in PBL', in Chen, S E, Cowdroy, R M, Kingsland, A J and Ostwald, M J (eds) *Reflections on Problem Based Learning*, Campbelltown, NSW, Australia: Problem Based Learning Network.

Saddington, T (1992) 'The use of learning contracts in higher education', in Brown, S and Baume, D (eds) *Learning Contracts: Volume One, A Theoretical Perspective, SCED Paper 71*, Birmingham: Standing Conference on Educational Development, 31–40.

Stephenson, J and Laycock, M (1993) 'Learning contracts: scope and rationale', in Stephenson, J and Laycock, M (eds) *Using Learning Contracts in Higher Education*, London: Kogan Page, 17–25.

Stephenson, J and Laycock, M (eds) (1993) *Using Learning Contracts in Higher Education*, London: Kogan Page.*

Tompkins, C and McGraw, M-J (1988) 'The negotiated learning contract', in Boud, D (ed.) *Developing Student Autonomy in Learning*, 2nd edn, London: Kogan Page, 172–91.

Learning contracts and specific courses

Information about the way learning contracts have been used in particular subjects or professional fields is useful for those who may wish to introduce them into their own courses. The following publications detail the processes involved in contract learning within specific courses or modules.

Arms, D, Chevevey, B, Karrer, C and Rumpler, C H (1984) 'A baccalaureate degree program in nursing for adult students', in Knowles, M S and Associates (eds) *Andragogy in Action*, San Francisco, CA: Jossey-Bass, 273–84.

Burns, S (1992) 'The stuff nightmares are made of or a useful way to learn nursing?' *Teaching News No. 32, Educational Methods Unit*, Oxford Brookes University, 18–20.

Cross, V (1992) *Using Learning Contracts in Clinical Education*, Birmingham: Queen Elizabeth School of Physiotherapy.

Fox, R D and West, R F (1983) 'Developing student competence in lifelong learning: the contract learning approach', *Medical Education*, 17, 247–53.

Hay-Smith, J (1993) 'Negotiating learning contracts for fieldwork placements in physiotherapy', in Stephenson, J and Laycock, M (eds) *Using Learning Contracts in Higher Education*, London: Kogan Page, 105–6.

Higgs, J and Boud, D J (1991) 'Self-directed learning as part of the mainstream of physiotherapy education', *Australian Journal of Physiotherapy*, 37, 249–55.

Hodgson, I (1993) 'Learning contracts for the industrial experience of hospitality management students', in Stephenson, J and Laycock, M (eds) *Using Learning Contracts in Higher Education*, London: Kogan Page, 107–14.

Hoffman, T (1986) 'Using learning contracts in HRD tertiary education', *Training and Development in Australia*, 13, 1, 11–12.

Kilpatrick, A C, Thompson, K H, Jarrett, H H and Anderson, R J (1984) 'Social work education at the University of Georgia', in Knowles, M S and Associates, *Andragogy in Action*, San Francisco, CA: Jossey-Bass, 243–63.

Martenson, D and Schwarb, P (1993) 'Learning by mutual committment: broadening the concept of learning contracts', *Medical Teacher*, 15, 1, 11–15.

Martes, K H (1981) 'Self-directed learning: an option for nursing education', *Nursing Outlook*, 29, 8, 472–7.

Moore, K (1993) 'The use of learning contracts in a self-managed learning MBA course', in Stephenson, J and Laycock, M (eds) *Using Learning Contracts in Higher Education*, London: Kogan Page, 134–9.

Nicholls, D (1992) 'Learning contracts in history projects by independent study', in Baume, D and Brown, S (eds) *Learning Contracts: Volume Two, Some Practical Examples*, SCED Paper 72, Birmingham: Standing Conference on Educational Development, 7–18.

Nicholls, D (1993) 'Using contracts in project placements', in Stephenson, J and Laycock, M (eds) *Using Learning Contracts in Higher Education*, London: Kogan Page, 89–96.

Ogbourne, W L and Killer, D V (1984) 'Learning by contract in family medicine training', *Family Practice*, 1, 2, 117–21.

Pratt, D and McGill, M K (1983) 'Educational contracts: the basis for effective clinical teaching', *Journal of Medical Education*, 58, 462–6.

Saunders, S and Gilpin, A (1988) 'Applying the learning contract model to communication courses in adult education', *Australian Communication Review*, 9, 4, 41–55.

Sloan, M and Schommer, B T (1975) 'The process of contracting in community nursing', in Spradley, B W (ed.) *Contemporary Community Nursing*, Boston, Mass: Little, Brown & Co.

Solomon, P (1992) 'Learning contracts in clinical education: evaluation by clinical supervisors', *Medical Teacher*, 14, 2/3, 205–10.

Learning contracts and work-based learning

One of the increasingly popular ways to use learning contracts is as a link between work experience and a formal course of study. Several accounts of how contracts have been used to plan, monitor and evaluate work experience programmes appear in recent publications.

Binns, R (1993) 'Development of capability, DTP and hypertext skills using learning contracts', in Stephenson, J and Laycock, M (eds) *Using Learning Contracts in Higher*

Education, London: Kogan Page, 67–9.

Boak, G and Stephenson, M (1987) 'Management learning contracts: from theory to practice', *Journal of European Industrial Training*, 11, 4, 4–6 and 11, 6, 17–20.

Brockbank, A (1993) 'Learning contracts and a company franchised programme', in Stephenson, J and Laycock, M (eds.) *Using Learning Contracts in Higher Education*, London: Kogan Page, 130–3.

Currie, D (1993) 'Custom-built learning contracts for corporate clients', in Stephenson, J and Laycock, M (eds) *Using Learning Contracts in Higher Education*, London: Kogan Page, 149–51.

Dare, C B (1984) 'Teaching nurses advanced skills at a metropolitan hospital', in Knowles, M S and Associates (eds) *Andragogy in Action*, San Francisco, CA: Jossey-Bass, 323–34.

Drew, S and Lawson, S (1993) 'Supporting the development of managerial competence using learning contracts', in Stephenson, J and Laycock, M (eds) *Using Learning Contracts in Higher Education*, London: Kogan Page, 70–4.

Gammie, E and Hornby, W (1994) 'Learning contracts and sandwich education', *Capability: The International Journal of Capability in Higher Education*, 1, 2, 46–58.

Harri-Augstein, S and Thomas, L (1993) 'Learning conversations and the personal learning contract: a methodology for enabling work-based learners to become more self-organised', in Stephenson, J and Laycock, M (eds) *Using Learning Contracts in Higher Education*, London: Kogan Page, 143–8.

Harris, C (1993) 'Institutional issues in the implementation of work-based learning contracts', in Stephenson, J and Laycock, M (eds) *Using Learning Contracts in Higher Education*, London: Kogan Page, 152–5.

Heie, H and Sweet, D (1984) 'Faculty development through growth contracts', in Knowles, M S and Associates, *Andragogy in Action*, San Francisco, CA: Jossey-Bass, 147–61.

Hinchcliffe, J (1993) 'The use of learning contracts for work-based management education and development', in Stephenson, J and Laycock, M (eds) *Using Learning Contracts in Higher Education*, London: Kogan Page, 140–2.

Houle, C O (1980) *Continuing Learning in the Professions*, San Francisco, CA: Jossey-Bass.

Marrington, P (1993) 'The learning contract as an aid to self-development and managerial competences', in Stephenson, J and Laycock, M (eds) *Using Learning Contracts in Higher Education*, London: Kogan Page, 75–9.

Marshall, I (1992) 'Using three-way learning contracts in work-based learning', in Baume, D and Brown, S (eds) *Learning Contracts: Volume Two, Some Practical Examples, SCED Paper 72*, Birmingham: Standing Conference on Educational Development, 53–6.

Marshall, I and Mill, M (1992) 'Learning contracts: how they can be used in work-based learning', in Mulligan, J and Griffin C (eds) *Empowerment through Experiential Learning*, London: Kogan Page, 211–21.

Marshall, I and Mill, M (1993) 'Using student-driven learning learning contracts in work-based learning and with small businesses', in Stephenson, J and Laycock, M (eds.) *Using Learning Contracts in Higher Education*, London: Kogan Page, 115–21.

Olivier, M and Mahoney, F (1984) 'Faculty orientation and in-service development at a State university system', in Knowles, M S and Associates, *Andragogy in Action*, San Francisco, CA: Jossey-Bass, 141–6.

Robertson, C (1993) 'Work-based learning contracts', in Stephenson, J and Laycock, M (eds) *Using Learning Contracts in Higher Education*, London: Kogan Page, 125–9.

Seymour, D (1988) 'Staff development by negotiated learning contract', *Industrial and Commercial Training*, 20, 6, 24–7.

Spaull, G (1993) 'The employer's perspective', in Stephenson, J and Laycock, M (eds) *Using Learning Contracts in Higher Education*, London: Kogan Page, 84–8.

Related learning and assessment issues

Learning contracts have arisen within a particular tradition of education and learning and are related to notions of independent study or self-directed learning. The titles below raise issues of relevance to the learning contract approach and expand upon some of the ideas presented in this book. These works present a wider perspective on the issues of learning and assessment raised earlier and some challenge the assumptions of self-directed learning.

Bates, I and Rowland S (1988) 'Is student-centred pedagogy "progressive" educational practice?' *Journal of Further and Higher Education*, 12, 3, 5–20.

Boomer, G, Lester, N, Onore, C and Cook, J (eds) (1992) *Negotiating the Curriculum: Education for the 21st. Century*, London: Falmer Press.

Boud, D (ed.) (1988) *Developing Student Autonomy in Learning*, 2nd edn, London: Kogan Page.

Boud, D (1992) 'The use of self-assessment schedules in negotiating learning', *Studies in Higher Education*, 17, 2, 185–200.

Boud, D (1995) 'Assessment and learning: contradictory or complementary?' in Knight, P (ed.) *Assessment for Learning in Higher Education*, London: Kogan Page, 35–48.

Boud, D and Higgs, J (1993) 'Bringing self-directed learning into the mainstream of tertiary education', in Graves, G (ed.) *Learner Managed Learning: Practice, Theory and Policy*, Leeds: World Education Fellowship and Higher Education for Capability, 158–73.

Brookfield, S (1984) 'Self-directed adult learning: a critical paradigm', *Adult Education Quarterly*, 35, 2, 59–71.

Brookfield, S (1985) *Self-Directed Learning: From Theory to Practice*, San Francisco, CA: Jossey-Bass.*

Brookfield, S (1986) *Understanding and Facilitating Adult Learning*, San Francisco, CA: Jossey-Bass.

Caffarella, R S and O'Donnell, J M (1987) 'Self-directed adult learning: a critical paradigm revisited', *Adult Education Quarterly*, 37, 4, 199–211.

Caffarella, R S and O'Donnell, J M (1991) 'Judging the quality of work-related, self-directed learning', *Adult Education Quarterly*, 42, 1, 17–29.

Candy, P (1987) 'Evolution, revolution or devolution: Increasing learner-control in the instructional setting', in Boud D and Griffin V (eds) *Appreciating Adults Learning: From the Learners' Perspective*, London: Kogan Page.

Candy, P (1988a) 'Key issues for research in self-directed learning, *Studies in Continuing Education*, 10, 104–24.

Candy, P (1988b) 'On the attainment of subject-matter autonomy', in Boud, D (ed.) *Developing Student Autonomy in Learning*, 2nd edn, London: Kogan Page, 59–76.

Candy, P (1991) *Self-Direction for Life-Long Learning: A Comprehensive Guide to Theory and Practice*, San Francisco, CA: Jossey-Bass.*

Edwards, R (1991) 'The politics of meeting learner needs: power, subject, subjection', *Studies in the Education of Adults*, 23, 1, 85–97.

Foley, G (1992) 'Self-directed learning', in Gonczi, A (ed.) *Developing a Competent Workforce*, Leabrook, South Australia.: National Centre for Vocational Education Research.

Galbraith, M W and Zelemark, B S (1991) 'Adult learning methods and techniques', in Galbraith, M W (ed.) *Facilitating Adult Learning*, Malabar, Fla: Krieger Publishing.

Grow, G O (1991) 'Teaching learners to be self-directed'. *Adult Education Quarterly*, 41, 3, 125–9.

Harber, C and Meighan, R (1986) 'A case study of democratic learning in teacher education', *Educational Review*, 38, 3, 273–82.

Hager, P and Gonczi, A (1991) 'Competency-based standards: a boon for continuing professional education?', *Studies in Continuing Education*, 13, 1, 24–40.

Hammond, M and Collins, R (1991) *Self-Directed Learning: Critical Practice*, London: Kogan Page.*

Harris, R (1989) 'Reflections on self-directed adult learning: some implications for educators of adults', *Studies in Continuing Education*, 11, 102–16.

Herman, R (ed.) (1982) *The Design of Self-Directed Learning: A Handbook for Teachers and Administrators*, Toronto: Ontario Institute for Studies in Education Press.

Knowles, M S (1980) *The Modern Practice of Adult Education: Andragogy versus Pedagogy*, New York: Association Press.

Knowles, M S (1990) *The Adult Learner: A Neglected Species*, 4th edn, Houston, Tex: Gulf Publishing.

Knowles, M S and Associates (1984) *Andragogy in Action*, San Francisco, CA: Jossey-Bass.*

Loacker, G and Doherty, A (1984) 'Self-directed undergraduate study', in Knowles, M S and

Associates (eds), *Andragogy in Action*, San Francisco, CA: Jossey-Bass, 101–19.

Millar, C, Morphet, T and Saddington, T (1986) 'Curriculum negotiation in professional adult education', *Journal of Curriculum Studies*, 18, 4, 429–43

Smith, R M (1983) *Learning How to Learn: Applied Theory for Adults*, Buckingham: Open University Press.

Stephenson, J (1988) 'The experience of independent study at North East London Polytechnic', in Boud, D (ed.) *Developing Student Autonomy in Learning*, 2nd edn, London: Kogan Page, 17–39.

Stephenson, J and Weil, S (1992) *Quality in Learning: A Capability Approach in Higher Education*, London: Kogan Page.

Withers, G and Cornish, G (1986) 'Non-competitive assessment: Its functions and its ideology', *Studies in Educational Evaluation*, 12, 3, 251–5.

Index